D1531611

BORN
under a
GOOD
SIGN

About the Author

Kristy Robinett is an over-achiever, over-sensitive, over-dramatized, over-sarcastic Scorpio. She's a psychic medium and author who began seeing spirits at the age of three. When she was eight, the spirit of her deceased grandfather helped her escape from a would-be kidnapper, and it was then that Robinett realized the Other Side wasn't so far away. As an adult, she was often called upon by the local police department to ex-

© E.C. Campbell Photography

amine cold cases in a new light and from a different angle. She gained a solid reputation for being extremely accurate at psychical profiling and giving new perspectives on unsolved crimes. It was then that she began working with a variety of law enforcement agencies, attorneys, and private investigators around the United States, aiding in missing persons, arson, and cold cases. In 2014 she appeared on a one-hour special on the Investigation Network (IN) called *Restless Souls*, spotlighting a police case she assisted on, and a television series in Japan.

Robinett teaches psychic development and paranormal investigating at local colleges, lectures across the country, and is a regular media commentator. She is the author of several books, including *Journey to the Afterlife*, *Tails from the Afterlife*, *It's a Wonderful Afterlife*, *Forevermore: Guided in Spirit by Edgar Allan Poe*, *Messenger Between Worlds: True Stories from a Psychic Medium*, *Higher Intuitions Oracle*, *Ghosts of Southeast Michigan*, and *Michigan's Haunted Legends and Lore*.

Kristy Robinett is a wife and mom to four adult kids and several animals. She enjoys gardening, cooking, and front porches. You can visit her online at KristyRobinett.com, facebook.com/kristyrobinett, or Twitter.com/kristyrobinett.

KRISTY
ROBINETT

BORN
under a
GOOD
SIGN

MAKE *the* MOST *of your*
ASTROLOGICAL SIGN

LLEWELLYN PUBLICATIONS
WOODBURY, MINNESOTA

Born Under a Good Sign: Make the Most of Your Astrological Sign © 2019 by Kristy Robinett. All rights reserved. No part of this book may be used or reproduced in any manner whatsoever, including internet usage, without written permission from Llewellyn Publications, except in the case of brief quotations embodied in critical articles and reviews.

FIRST EDITION
First Printing, 2019

Book design: Samantha Penn
Cover design: Shira Atakpu

Llewellyn Publications is a registered trademark of Llewellyn Worldwide Ltd.

Library of Congress Cataloging-in-Publication Data (Pending)
ISBN: 978-0-7387-5716-2

Llewellyn Worldwide Ltd. does not participate in, endorse, or have any authority or responsibility concerning private business transactions between our authors and the public.

All mail addressed to the author is forwarded but the publisher cannot, unless specifically instructed by the author, give out an address or phone number.

Any internet references contained in this work are current at publication time, but the publisher cannot guarantee that a specific location will continue to be maintained. Please refer to the publisher's website for links to authors' websites and other sources.

Llewellyn Publications
A Division of Llewellyn Worldwide Ltd.
2143 Wooddale Drive
Woodbury, MN 55125-2989
www.llewellyn.com

Printed in the United States of America

Other Books by Kristy Robinett

*It's a Wonderful Afterlife: Inspiring
True Stories from a Psychic Medium*

*Journey to the Afterlife: Comforting Messages
& Lessons from Loved Ones in Spirit*

*Tails from the Afterlife: Stories of Signs,
Messages & Inspiration from your
Animal Companions*

*Messages From a Wonderful Afterlife:
Signs Loved Ones Send from Beyond*

*Messenger Between Worlds:
True Stories from a Psychic Medium*

*Forevermore: Guided in
Spirit by Edgar Allan Poe*

*To those who believe in the magic of the moon
and the wisdom of the stars.*

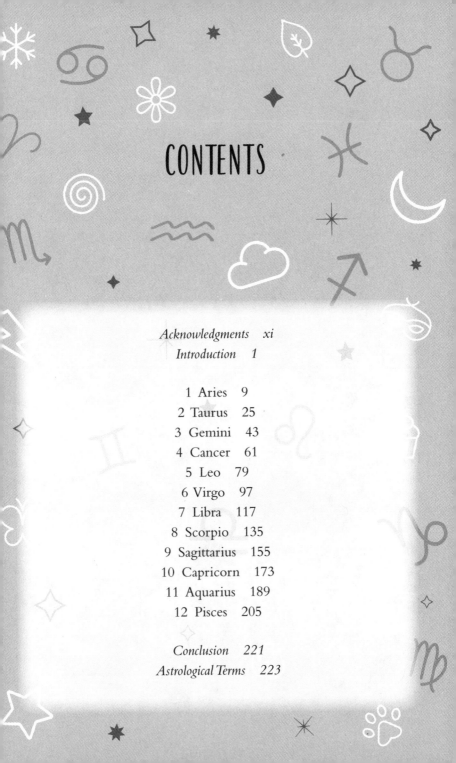

CONTENTS

ACKNOWLEDGMENTS

Donna was one of my very first clients when I opened my private practice. Although I was taught business should never be mixed with my personal life, it was hard not to let Donna into my life. That spunky Sagittarius quickly became my very best friend. In June 2018, my Donna unexpectedly made her journey home to the other side. I haven't deleted her voicemails or her emails, but whenever I need to hear a taste of Donna, I listen to her directly. Through her loving but very practical advice, Donna Shorkey was my biggest fan and cheerleader, and I'll forever miss her every single day.

I'm honored by the always and forever support and unconditional love of my Pisces husband Chuck Robinett and my children Micaela Even Kempf (Leo), Caleb Kempf (Virgo), Connor Even (Aries), Serenity (Aries), Cora Kutnick (Aquarius), and Molly Robinett (Leo).

To my dad and Scorpio birthday buddy, Ronald Schiller. And the very sassy Taurus mother-in-law, Mary Lou. Fly high with the angels, mom.

Mikey (Leo) and Marjanna McClain (Aries), our travel buddies, who so lovingly help us with events, late-night laughs, and constant adventures—I pray we have decades of more fun.

Thanks to Mary Byberg, my assistant and friend, who's an artist extraordinaire, and a sassy and ever-patient Gemini.

Thank you also to my friends Gayle Buchan, Rosalyn Mastrangelo, Katie Eaves, Colleen and Dennis Kwieciński, Courtney Sieira, Candace Isaacson, and Leslie and Andy Cirinesi.

Thanks to my paranormal investigation team Jan Tomes, Kathy Curatolo, Lynn Bowers, and Ryan Sparks for their friendship and Scooby Doo escapades. Who knew that sitting in the dark talking to spirits and ghosts would bring about such a close friendship and family?

This book would have never come to life if it weren't for my friends at Llewellyn Worldwide. To Amy Glaser, who is always available to be Oprah and Doctor Phil to me when I'm pulling my hair out and doubting my writing abilities. Thank you for helping my writing appear like a semi-intelligent person wrote it. Also, thanks to Anna Levine and Bill Krause for supporting me through my crazy suggestions for topics.

And finally, I thank my clients and social media friends for their continued support and love. I believe in you—the thousands of clients and their loved ones on the other side who have touched my life more than I could ever eloquently communicate. For their stories and the connections that never get old. I'm grateful every day and feel blessed.

INTRODUCTION

We shouldn't be ruled by our horoscope or second-guess our relationships according to the astrological signs. There is, however, a clarity and practical solution when understanding the energy of each zodiac sign. With that greater understanding you can facilitate a better future for yourself and learn how to surround yourself with people to help you, and you them, become healthier and happier as well.

Astrological Rebel

While most kids would open the newspaper to the funny pages, I was sneaking a peek at the horoscopes. My mom would hiss at the ridiculous idea that every Virgo, or Scorpio, or Aries could possibly have the exact same kind of day or future.

"We have free will," she would say. "It's your choice to have a good or a bad day, not what the author of the horoscopes decided your day would be."

I agreed with my mom, but I was captivated. It's not as if I was punished by my parents if I read the horoscopes, but it wasn't allowed either. The astrological rebel in me did it anyway.

My interest in the zodiac continued into college, and much of my psychology paperwork revolved around astrology, energy, and mediumship. I was excited to find a flyer on my campus for a class that explored the world of astrology and how it impacted everyday life. I'd carried the experience and the energy with me through my every day, without anybody to truly talk to or be mentored by. Without telling anyone, especially my parents, I signed up for the weekend class.

The class wasn't about spouting factoids; instead we dove into the attributes and quirks of our fellow zodiacs. There weren't notes, only experiences. We learned about the zodiac signs, planets, moons, rising signs, aspects, elements, and how to complete and interpret birthcharts; but the teacher's mystical beliefs were anything but standard. Although maybe not so original, we were taught that astrology wasn't the only thing to look at. Aside from astrology, there was the I Ching, Myers-Briggs Type Indicator, Keirsey Temperament Sorter, iPersonic Personality Type, and other personality tests to help with a baseline, but mostly it came down to trusting the energy and following through with the intuition.

Astrological Inspirations

The Western world considers astrology a pseudo-science, while the Eastern world utilizes astrology for decisions, predictions, and reflections on everything from marriage to job opportunities.

Neither astrology nor energy is something you need to believe in. Just like you don't need to believe in the sun: It will still shine. So does the energy of astrology.

Everything has an ebb and flow of energy—its own personal vibration. Everything vibrates at one speed, or another speed. Although you may not see the vibrations, many feel the vibrations or frequency. If you've ever met someone and immediately loved them from just a small conversation, or if you've ever met someone and immediately disliked them from just a small conversation, then you felt their vibration, and it either matched or didn't match yours.

Although astrology isn't science, it is inspiration. You'll discover that the people you embrace, the jobs you choose, even the clothes you buy, are all a part of who you are. We each have our own individual energy, much like a fingerprint. Add to that the energy of influences, and then there's the foundation of our astrological sign that creates yet another layer—kind of like the cherry on the top of the sundae. Some people focus on just the cherry, but there's so much more to investigate. A soul-coaching appointment I facilitated with a lovely couple helped to explain just that.

Arka and Bansi sat across from me, holding hands.

"Both of your dads are standing next to you in spirit," I offered. "You two are soul mates, that's what they tell me. Yet they tell me you are having doubts. It's that doubt that is tripping up your life."

My male client, Bansi, sighed heavily and grabbed his wife's hand before taking another deep breath and beginning. "We don't doubt our relationship, but our Hindu priest did our astrological chart and we were determined to be incompatible. He would not marry us. So we married here in the United States."

"A sin," his father told me in spirit. "A sin according to our family and our beliefs. But tell them I see that although there are problems, there will always be some problems. He knows," the spirit laughed. "He knows his mother and I had a stellar chart and yet had a very disruptive and exhausting marriage."

I shared the information, and the couple both laughed.

Arka's father then lovingly shared, "We've discovered that the chart is truly a guideline, not a Bible. It doesn't necessarily protect you from the rough waters but helps steer you out of the storm. You can listen to the weather report or ignore it."

"So they aren't mad at us?" Arka asked, tears forming in her eyes.

I shook my head no after the confirmation from their dads.

Not every Gemini is incompatible with a Pisces, even though the books say so. Not every Leo will get a job promotion during Venus rising.

Always trust your intuition even if you don't know why. Always use your inner knowledge; don't make knowledge fit. A person's energy isn't exact to what is on paper; sometimes it's in front of you to uncover.

Decans

Have you ever wondered why you never felt like you fit the description of the stereotype of your astrological sign? Most don't realize that the astrological signs are each divided by their elements, qualities, and masculine and feminine expressions. One of the thumbprints is connected to the astrological decan. While we each have our own sun sign, each of those sun signs are divided into subgroups, divided into roughly ten-day periods, called decans. Each decan holds its own personality trait, which digs deeper into the general zodiac sign. The horoscopes printed in a newspaper or magazine lumps these decans into one under that sign, and sometimes it's just not accurate. Yet sometimes it is.

Horoscopes have always fascinated me, but I took them with a grain of salt. It wasn't until I began to study the sun signs and characteristics that I saw there were patterns. Not identical, but an outline connected to the energy of each sun sign. It wasn't until I embraced my mediumship that I realized we each have an energy, a spiritual thumbprint, and within that thumbprint are traits that come from our astrological sign. We don't, however, take on all of them. If your mom and dad are both Capricorns, one might be strong-willed and confident, while the other might be depressed and scared. It doesn't mean that the one doesn't fit the Capricorn traits, though. One picked up some of the energy, while the other picked up another vibration. Add in masculine energy, or feminine energy, neither of which is gender-based, and the decans, and you begin to build the whole picture of that individual.

Triplicities

The division of the decans is called the triplicities, with energy taken from fire, earth, air, and water. Each zodiac sign governs 30 degrees of the natal chart. Twelve zodiac signs at 30 degrees each constitute the complete natal chart encompassing 360 degrees. Each sign is divided into three divisions of 10 degrees, and each sign has three decans, one for each division of 10 degrees. Each decan has a ruler, which becomes the sub ruler of the sign or the coruler of the sign, and it is a wonderful influence.

Spiritual Thumbprints

We also have other energy traits that complement and complicate our sun sign. Like a layer of the thumbprint, our prints are formed in the womb, and our spiritual traits are as well. And like a thumbprint that never changes but does grow with our growing body, our spiritual traits shift through our experiences and relationships. Those traits are many and sometimes complex, ebbing and flowing with our life experiences and relationships. Being an introvert, an extrovert, an empath, or a risk taker affects all sorts of relationships.

You've met one Scorpio therefore you've met them all, right? We know this isn't true at all. Those who have twins truly understand that assumption to be false. Those born under the same zodiac signs are different by nature, by what we refer to as energy or a spiritual personality. We are born with our very own spiritual thumbprint, which includes a variety of tools to help. I've discovered through my years of energy work and research into astrology that there are constant doorways to open—a quest of constant knowledge to help better relationship practices and leadership capabilities.

The Moon and Its Phases

As the moon travels through the signs, the positive and negative effects of that sign's energy will affect you during the new and Full Moon phases, no matter your sun sign. A New Moon, or Dark Moon since you won't see any moon, occurs once a month. The New Moon is the darkest phase of the moon, but it also marks the beginning of the two-week time frame when the moon moves away from the sun and increases in light, which is a great time to begin new projects, new love, new careers, or anything else new you want to do (or are afraid to do).

The Full Moon is bright and radiant and provides an excellent time to look at your life and let go of what is not serving you, and to wrap up projects and move on. It's a wonderful time to do some soul work and face facts, no matter how uncomfortable. The energy a few days beforehand and a few days after a Full Moon tends to be unstable. It can affect you and others emotionally and sometimes even physically. Weather disasters and natural disasters are quite common during this time, so don't be surprised when you see some heavy news.

Endless Doorways

I was employed in the human resource field for more than twenty years, all the while using astrology, energy, and management insight to help create successful practices. So often we forget that this practice isn't woo-woo and it can be used in the mainstream.

Although I've retired my corporate human resource hat and now, by day, I'm a professional psychic medium, I'm also a life coach who offers soul guidance. Helping my clients to overcome their fears and obstacles in an individual, group, or corporate setting has been a passion of mine, especially when it includes all I've learned.

In the middle of an economic downfall, when my astrological chart told me *not* to quit my day job, I bucked the system and the horoscopes and quit my day job to open an office as a psychic medium, author, and inspirational speaker. My friend, an attorney by day and an astrologer by night, warned me that my planets, houses, moons, and transitions weren't aligned for a positive outcome. To me, though, it felt right. Was it simple luck, or trusting the energy and intuition that helped me land on my own two feet instead of smashing my face into the proverbial celestials?

Mine Is Better Than Yours

I utilize astrology the same way I do my intuition—knowing that it's a gauge that never lies, but our assumptions fib something fierce. Just because you dated a terrible Leo doesn't mean that all Leos are terrible. Just because your best friend is a fabulous Capricorn doesn't mean that all Capricorns are fabulous. There's so much more to mere astrology than what meets the eye. Reading the jacket of the book doesn't give you the full content, and neither do the zodiac stereotypes.

"What's your sign?" is a tongue-in-cheek pickup line. I've found most people know what their astrological sign is, and they believe their sign is better than all others, offering the reason why. Sometimes they even include their negative attributes with pride, like a badge of astrological honor. There are no bad signs, just bad people that make those signs look bad. What is the best sign? They're all good signs!

This book will strip away the astrological woo-woo, without fancy charts or planet, moon, and star chatter. There are sensible and healing explanations that will give you a handbook with a deeper perception in dealing with anyone—from a parent, child, partner, or boss—according to the energy of their astrological sun sign. It's been said that there's no handbook for life; this should help demystify the astrological myths and show you that we're all born under a good sign.

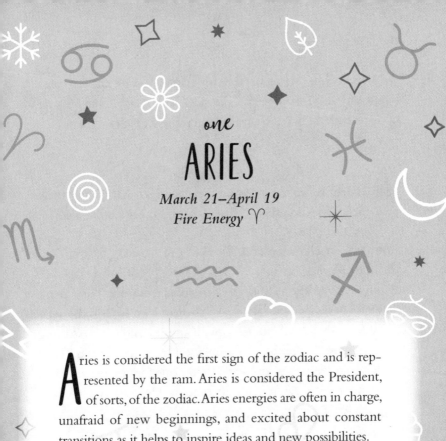

one
ARIES

March 21–April 19
Fire Energy ♈

ries is considered the first sign of the zodiac and is represented by the ram. Aries is considered the President, of sorts, of the zodiac. Aries energies are often in charge, unafraid of new beginnings, and excited about constant transitions as it helps to inspire ideas and new possibilities.

Aries loves to be number one, and they show it by their boldness and ambitious ways. With their ram-like sign, they dive headfirst into challenging situations with chess game strategies. Aries is a passionate, motivated, and confident leader who is determined and direct. They like situations that are emotionally clean, and they are not afraid to roll up their sleeves to make it that way; but they will tire if someone else isn't carrying their weight.

Aries is strong and sometimes militant-minded. They don't like people telling them what to do, but love telling others how to do it.

9

Aries energies are often taken for granted because they are very kind-hearted. When they love, they love with their all, and because of that a betrayal or backstab is excruciatingly tough on them.

Aries Decans

Each zodiac is broken down into triplicities, each having their own energy added to their zodiac sign. This is Aries broken down:

Aries of First Decan: March 21–30
Ruled by Mars.

Positive Energy Traits: Enthusiastic and adventurous. They aren't afraid of danger and often take chances. This Aries is the type of friend who will come up with an idea, and the next thing you know, you're strapped into a seat in the craziest and scariest rollercoaster in the state. Being ruled by Mars, this Aries moves forward, although sometimes recklessly.

Negative Energy Traits: They can be argumentative. They get frustrated easily and can sometimes come across as lazy. This is the type of child who will pout and turn into a limp noodle when they can't get their way, and will mope and whine the entire time because it wasn't their idea. As an adult, you will likely see them glaring in their cubicle after their idea wasn't picked up.

Aries of Second Decan: March 31–April 9
Ruled by the Sun.

Positive Energy Traits: Ambitious, caring, humanitarian, and focused. You'll likely find this Aries raking the leaves for their neighbors, volunteering at the animal shelter, baking cookies for the bake sale, and taking on eighteen credits of classes. There is no lack of energy. Being ruled by the Sun makes this Aries consistent, loyal, and determined with a side of fiery intensity.

Negative Energy Traits: They keep their feelings to themselves, and sometimes that can come across as smug and conceited to those who don't know them. It's hard for this Aries to open up to others—even those they know and trust.

Aries of Third Decan: April 10–20
Ruled by Jupiter.

Positive Energy Traits: Intelligent and strong-willed. They are independent and bold. This Aries is driven by their positive attitude and an unlimited confidence that makes them a natural-born leader who will push boundaries. Being ruled by Jupiter, this Aries believes everything bigger is better.

Negative Energy Traits: Often brash and demanding, even to those they love. They want everything done the way they see to be right. This Aries doesn't always elegantly communicate what their right way entails and can come across as condescending.

March Aries vs. April Aries

Along with each sign being split into their third decans, there is a difference between each zodiac split between the months.

The March Aries loves to have others do the work.

The April Aries is a hard worker.

The March Aries is impulsive.

The April Aries thinks things through.

The March Aries is hardheaded.

The April Aries is feisty.

The March Aries bucks the system.

The April Aries likes justice.

The March Aries is creative.
The April Aries is a creative thinker.
The March Aries is a problem maker.
The April Aries is a problem solver.
The March Aries is emotional.
The April Aries tries to hide their emotions.

Aries Masculine and Feminine Energy

Energy has a yin and yang that is interpreted as feminine and masculine, and according to the energy it is explained below:

Feminine March Aries: The feminine energy of a March Aries is very sensitive, intuitive, and loving. They get frustrated and overwhelmed easily, trying to please everyone and often forgetting about taking care of themselves.

Masculine March Aries: The masculine energy of a March Aries is creative, logical, and complicated. They can be vindictive and manipulative, charismatic, and arrogant.

Feminine April Aries: The feminine energy of an April Aries is smart, funny, but sometimes naïve. They want to believe in the good in everybody, sometimes putting too much into taking care of everyone else.

Masculine April Aries: The masculine energy of an April Aries likes life to be as uncomplicated as possible. Pretty much if you say and do everything the way they believe it should be, then they believe life would be perfect. A bit militant, they want things itinerized and organized—mostly emotionally, but physically too.

Aries Positive Traits

Logical/Practical
Aries energies are straight-forward thinkers and doers. An Aries doesn't waste their time overthinking. They trust their intuition and make sure to focus on the job at hand rather than looking in the past for regrets or worrying about the what-ifs.

Enterprising
The Aries energy is a perpetual mediator. They work hard at trying to change what they are told they can't change. That persistence and strong will can be negative but can also be positive, depending upon how they channel it. Aries has an overwhelming energy to take on big tasks and finish them on time, although it might be in the eleventh hour.

Independent
Maybe it's because Aries is the first sign of the zodiac that makes them believe they must be the leader and in charge. They don't love the idea of anyone telling them what to do; they'd rather figure it out all on their own, whether it is successful or a flop.

Aries Negative Traits

Impatient
Arian energies get bored and impatient if things don't happen right now, in their own Aries timeline. Their life needs to be filled with spirited experiences to keep their minds busy.

Argumentative
Aries is ruled by the red, angry, fearless planet Mars, so it's no wonder that an Aries will always win their argument. The fiery

Aries rarely shies away from a dispute and will go above and beyond to prove that they are right and everyone else is wrong, even if they are wrong.

Arrogant

It's easy to see the arrogance in an Aries, especially if you attempt to correct one—even through constructive criticism. Even if they are wrong, they would rather cover their tracks than admit any wrongdoing.

Aries Keywords

Aries Communication Style

An Aries needs detailed specifics. Simple yes or no questions will easily bore an Aries. An engaged conversation that is direct is best. An Aries is literally minded. Vague instructions or information will frustrate an Aries and shut them down. You can't simply ask them to get your glasses off the table, you must describe what the table looks like, in what part of the room it is, and then describe the glasses in detail too.

An Aries isn't fond of leaving voice messages and would prefer the call is answered immediately, or the text message responded to right then. The ram will move on quickly otherwise. Time is precious to the Aries, and if you respect that you gain future respect.

Aries Misconceptions

An Aries isn't sensitive

There is a misconception that an Aries isn't sensitive, with their logical and pragmatic personality. However, many Aries energies are what is called an empath. They love to help others, but they also love to help others who want to help themselves. The Aries energy often works so hard at being portrayed as strong, holding up everyone else up like a leader should, that their sensitive side isn't recognized, and yet it is there, especially to those closest to them.

Don't Be an Aries, Aries

Aries, you love to be competitive and the leader—all the time. We know you don't play well with others and most times you dismiss others' opinions or ideas because you are so busy trying to be right. The lesson for you is to stop trying so hard; stop and listen to what others have to say, too, so that you don't make impulsive, rash, and hot-headed decisions.

Thoughts from an Aries

An Aries is no-nonsense, and life will go more smoothly if everyone sees it the way that an Aries sees it.

> "You can put water on me to calm me. Or you can really ignite me and make a blaze. I am a well-tempered person and I handle things calmly, that is until I don't, and then I start to feel a little fire starting. People can help with water to calm my nerves down or they can add to the problem and make things worse. I do have tendencies to be an introvert—I'm not good in crowds and do not like to be around a whole bunch of people at one time. However, if you come to my space and my territory, I wake up to become me and you will love me. I also believe in my intuitions."
>
> —Amy

Keep It Moving

The Aries is first and believes in moving forward rather than sitting still, and they won't wait for you to catch up either.

> "An Aries has a reputation for being stubborn, hardheaded, impatient, and opinionated. For the most part, this is an accurate statement dependent on what part of the Aries sign you're born in. The beginning, the middle, or the end will determine to what degree you display these wonderful features. We are loyal, sometimes to a fault, and demand loyalty in return. Loyalty failure results in the infamous 'Irish goodbye'—we don't look back. We move forward on to bigger and better things.

We tend to be labeled as arrogant, but we consider it confidence. People say we are aggressive, yet to us we are assertive. People say we are hot-headed. Well then, don't piss us off. We are the FIRST sign in the zodiac for a reason. Competitive Aries will do her best to be number one in everything she does."

—Deb

Leadership

Aries takes being the first sign in the zodiac very seriously and feel they must be the leader in everything.

"I am a leader, not a follower. I perform well under pressure. I can be very stubborn and headstrong. I am very competitive and ambitious, I do not like to lose, and I do not like to be wrong. When I know I am right I will argue to the bitter end and I will always have the last word. I can be very companionate and passionate about things that are important to me. When I care about someone, I will go to the ends of earth for them. I am driven and determined as well, especially if I must overcome obstacles."

—Bobbie

Aries and Relationships

A relationship with an Aries is hardly dull. They love adventure and romance. They are planners and take the reins. An Aries is faithful and loyal and will be insulted if a partner shows jealousy. The March energy Aries is often moodier than those born in April.

Strengths

The Aries is loyal and will protect you to the end. No matter, you can count on an Aries to stand by your side and be a constant cheerleader. An Aries isn't into playing games with a love relationship or friendship and will make it clear where they stand.

Challenges

An Aries must have it go their way, and this can seem controlling and temperamental. Despite the Aries looking tough and stable, they are fragile and easily hurt. They have a hard time forgiving and hardly ever forget, which can build up resentment and tall walls.

Aries in the Workplace

Strengths

Your Aries boss or coworker is a natural leader, being ambitious, energetic, and competitive. Aries people are fair and just want the same for those they respect. They will defend those they respect with their utmost dedication.

The Aries boss will respect those who demonstrate professionalism. They make great leaders and know how to insightfully look at how to mentally challenge their employees.

Challenges

An Aries doesn't automatically trust and respect; instead, these traits must be gained in a professional way. Aries are wonderful at arguing in a pragmatic way, so be cautious when confronting an Aries that you have all your facts straight. Their horns are sharp.

Parenting an Aries Child

An Aries child loves to be the leader, so give them specific responsibilities with a set allowance and instructions of how to save and spend. The Aries child loves to have some money in their pocket.

Strengths

Positive: If you have an Aries personality, you have a naturally positive, energetic, and happy approach, which the highly energetic Aries child will hugely benefit from. You can expect many happy days connecting to your child through fun and happy emotions, as even the smallest things will result in big smiles.

Natural Leaders: The Aries child is competitive and loves a challenge, which leads to being a wonderful leader. They don't love others telling them what to do but will listen and be respectful.

Busy: Both a strength and a challenge; the Aries wants to be involved in everything possible—from guitar lessons to soccer and everything in between. They love to stay active morning, noon, and night.

Generous: The Aries is a wonderful sibling and friend, sharing what they have, whether it be their juice box or their newest video game.

Challenges

Sensitive: Aries children can be extremely sensitive, but they need a healthy balance of space and parenting.

Prone to Withdraw: They can withdraw during adversity, and the more you press them to talk about it, the more withdrawn they will become, even moving their anger over to an innocent party that wants to help.

Stubborn: March Aries are good at being manipulative, stubborn, and argumentative.

Pressure: April Aries put a lot of pressure on themselves and others, sometimes setting themselves up for disappointment.

Aries as a Parent

Ambitious: An Aries parent is a hard worker, wanting everything to be perfect from the pregnancy to the college fund. They are determined to champion the job of being a parent and making an example out of their ambition.

Meticulous: Everything is done in a meticulous way, without leaving a lot of wiggle room.

Wanderlust: An Aries parent loves to travel and doesn't hesitate to take their kids on extravagant vacations. They also don't hesitate to have someone else take care of the kids so that they can go on a child-free vacation.

Rule Keepers: There are rules, and then there are Aries rules. They want their child(ren) to know their place by offering guidelines with bluntness and direct honesty. A rebellious child that likes to color outside the lines can make this is a tumultuous relationship.

Competitors: One of the most competitive energies, an Aries parent wants to be the best at their job and wants their child(ren) to do the same. The kids are often signed up for every activity and pushed to do their best at it all. Aries likes to see their kids succeed without micromanaging too much.

Strengths

Efficient: Aries parents love to create rules in order to keep an efficient household. They'd rather parent a child that doesn't need micromanaging, as their own lives are often kept busy.

Nurturing: They are nurturing and loving, but their compassion is often behind some tough layers. Although an Aries parent isn't warm and fuzzy, they are loving, and they do offer independent thinking and a lot of energy.

Challenges

Communication Issues: Aries parents love their children unconditionally, but they may not openly communicate their feelings.

More Work Than Play: An Aries parent pushes, especially with academics in order to help their child(ren) with future opportunities, but sometimes the Aries parent forgets that the child needs to play too.

Aries and Finances

Aries love their money. They also like to spend money. A March Aries may find themselves in trouble, while an April Aries will be saving (or thinking about it) for their retirement at an early age. With the fire power that Aries can embrace, it can make them an unstoppable force of nature. Sometimes, though, there can be some impulsive and reckless spending. Aries energies do best with the structure of a financial planner and learning how to build their portfolio early on.

Moon in Aries

New Moon in Aries

A New Moon, or Dark Moon since you won't see any moon, occurs once a month. The New Moon is the darkest phase of the Moon, but it also marks the beginning of the two-week time frame when the Moon moves away from the Sun and increases in light, which is a great time to begin new projects, new love, new careers, or anything else new you want to do (or are afraid to do)!

This Aries energy makes it a wonderful time to look at long-term plans in your life. It's a good time for working on releasing past issues by allowing them to bubble over and then letting go. Feel and then release. Think of it from an exercise standpoint: You must first warm up or you may get hurt during the most intense routine. If you don't allow the cooldown, the same can occur. And if you are just going through the warm-up and not allowing the actual workout to happen, you don't get results. Don't get caught up in the cycle of what isn't good for you and allow the past to consume you.

This energy helps you refind your confidence and power, making it a wonderful time to begin a new career, projects, or love interests.

You might find that the fire you thought had fizzled out of you has instead reignited. This moon phase burns with a fury. You will more than likely be less than patient with those who display an entitled attitude and are even vocal about it. Obviously, be careful. Sure, you may believe what you think and what you say but know that saying it cannot change it and therefore the best energy may be spent by walking away.

This energy makes it a wonderful time to look at long-term plans in your life.

What You May See during the Aries New Moon Phase:
>A feeling of anger.
>A new-found confidence.
>More intense weather patterns.
>A feeling that you need to get moving in your life.
>Some anxiety and impatience over where you are and
>>where you want to be.
>More spirit/ghost sightings.
>People acting more assertive (traffic, lines, at work, etc.).
>Pets acting out of sorts.

Full Moon in Aries

Aries is a spunky energy. During this moon phase you will more than likely feel braver than you have in a long time. This is the time to take thought-out chances and risks that will help you create more independence in your life. Remember that thoughts create things, so even the smallest change can make a huge shift.

Soul Work

Write down ten things that you want to stop in your life and then rip up or burn them, and then write down ten things that you do want in your life and focus on that! The Full Moon helps you get closer to the end game of all the hard work you've put in.

Now Is the Time

Do take a chance. Don't assume anything. Do talk to the person if you are upset instead of festering in the muck. Don't suppress your feelings. Do start planning your future.

Aries Totem Animal

Hawk

In some Native American cultures the hawk is the messenger. It shows up when we need to pay attention to the subtle messages found around us, within us, and in the ethereal realms. It has an overall message of looking for the truth within and around your life, recognizing that which is felt and might be seen. It's no wonder that hawks are the protectors and visionaries of the Air. They hold a high responsibility and the Aries feels that same burden. But just like the hawk, the Aries energy is rarely afraid of taking initiative and going after what they want. They learn early on that they can rest (briefly), roost, and recharge.

The hawk offers a gift of:

Clear-sightedness

Courage

Independence

Loyalty

Opportunity

Focus

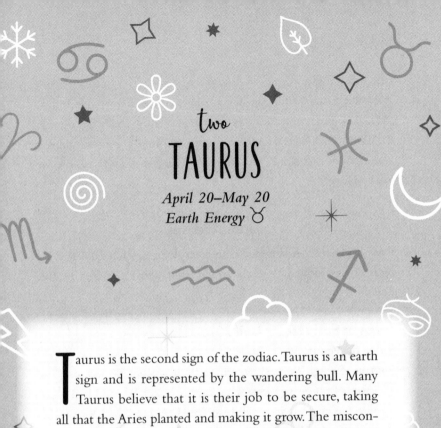

two

TAURUS

April 20–May 20
Earth Energy ♉

aurus is the second sign of the zodiac. Taurus is an earth sign and is represented by the wandering bull. Many Taurus believe that it is their job to be secure, taking all that the Aries planted and making it grow. The misconception of the Taurus is that they are stubborn like the bull their astrological sign represents. While strong will can be a trait (especially when angry), a Taurus is overall very gentle, loving, and loyal, and will bend over backward for those they love—they just don't want to be taken for granted. When that occurs, they show you that bull-like temper and forgiveness doesn't come easily.

Taurus energy is all about hard work and reliability. This energy takes work, financial situations, and life very seriously, and they put a lot of pressure on themselves. Taurean energy likes the nicer things in life and will make the extra effort to insure those. Often practical and pragmatic (sometimes to a fault), they just don't play well with *stupid* people or those who lack common sense. And they especially have a lack of tolerance around those who don't pull their weight. No matter the challenge, though, the Taurus will take it on. But watch out, there's often moodiness and anxiety that shines through, even though they think they've masked it well.

Taurus Decans

Each zodiac is broken down into triplicities, each having their own energy added to their zodiac sign. This is Taurus broken down:

Taurus of First Decan: April 20–30
Ruled by Venus.

Positive Energy Traits: Determined and stable. A mediator and lover of peace and love. This Taurus is soft-hearted and wears just the right shade of rose-colored glasses. They love to indulge in all things that would use their five senses. Whether it's enchanting aromas, delicious foods, amazing vacations, or a gentle touch, they love to share in the experiences with those they love.

Negative Energy Traits: This Taurus has trouble adjusting to new ideas and situations, unless it comes from their own suggestions. They can get stuck in their own comfort zone and habits and be unmovable with what anyone else wants in that moment. This Taurus loves to love the best of the best, and it often comes with buyer's remorse and having to quickly figure out the finances.

Taurus of Second Decan: May 1–10
Ruled by Mercury.

Positive Energy Traits: This Taurus loves to communicate their thoughts and feelings. They are charming, thoughtful, tactful, and loving. If your mom was rushed to the hospital, this Taurus would show up and wait with you. Knee deep in a home project? This Taurus would get their overalls on, but not before YouTubing to see how to do the said project and coming with all the tools and expertise.

Negative Energy Traits: Can sometimes come across as shy or aloof. Often overly realistic and pragmatic, especially with finances. This Taurus often takes on more than they can chew, and they are met with chaos and confusion trying to time-manage themselves at the last minute.

Taurus of Third Decan: May 11–21
Ruled by Saturn.

Positive Energy Traits: Loyal, disciplined, and steady. Caring and mostly patient, this Taurus is hardworking and would prefer to make their own ladder, figure out how to make it as balanced and steady as possible, so they, themselves, can climb it without anyone helping. They will happily celebrate their own hustle and perseverance with beaming pride.

Negative Energy Traits: This Taurus has an unusual sense of humor that only some may understand. They have a stable and grounded personality that some may view as boring and dull. They are a bit of a taskmaster, requiring everyone to be on the same page as them at the same time; otherwise their stress shows bright.

April Taurus vs. May Taurus

Along with each sign being split into their third decans, there is a difference between each zodiac split between the months.

The April Taurus is pragmatic and practical.

The May Taurus pretends they are pragmatic and practical.

The April Taurus is laid back.

The May Taurus is wound tight.

The April Taurus is shy with regard to romance.

The May Taurus is flirtatious.

The April Taurus can be rude, especially when things aren't going their way.

The May Taurus is great with silent treatments.

The April Taurus is sweet.

The May Taurus can be arrogant.

The April Taurus is afraid of hurting others' feelings.

The May Taurus runs away so as not to have to deal with others' feelings.

Taurus Masculine and Feminine Energy

Energy has a yin and yang that is interpreted as feminine and masculine, and according to the energy it is explained below:

Feminine April Taurus: The feminine energy of a Taurus in April is confident, intelligent, and determined. They may pretend to be tougher than they are, but they are very compassionate and nurturing. They don't like to be wrong and will fib to make themselves look more right than they really are.

Masculine April Taurus: The masculine energy of a Taurus in April was born to be a leader. They are career-oriented and strong-willed. Although they may come across as tough and emotionally detached, they are very romantic and thoughtful; you simply have to win them over with your truthfulness and vulnerability and they will respond accordingly.

Feminine May Taurus: The feminine Taurus in May is a powerhouse. They are exactly who they show you they are. Emotional, empathic, and loyal, the feminine Taurus in May shares their sweetness with everyone—just don't backstab them because they will cut you off and not think twice.

Masculine May Taurus: The masculine Taurus in May try. They don't always try hard, though, and can be perceived as lazy. It's not necessarily that they want to lie on the couch and not do anything, or tinker on their laptop or game unit; it's sometimes their escape from their anxiety. They really don't want everyone to see all of them, and they can be temperamental. They are competitive with themselves. They are romantic and thoughtful when they let you get close to them.

Taurus Positive Traits

Dependable

The bull is one of the most solid in the zodiac. The Taurus will jump at the chance to help anyone and go above and beyond. For example, if you're moving, a Taurus won't bail on you; instead, they will rent the best moving truck for you and delegate a plan of efficiency and time management.

Intellectual

You will likely find a Taurus with their tablet, phone, and laptop nearby at the same time. Although they will play a game here or there, they'd rather gain information about whatever they can soak up. One site may be open to the word of the day while the other is a YouTube video on how to work on their car engine, and the other is a recipe on how to brine the best turkey. The Taurus isn't afraid to take on new responsibilities, sign up for classes, or learn whatever it is they need to or whatever sparks their interest. The Taurus never lacks an endless mental cabinet of knowledge.

Hardworking

The Taurus is hardworking, loyal, and practical. They prefer stability and security, which makes them loyal employees, bosses, friends, and partners. The Taurus has an entrepreneurial mind and they know how to calmly deal with issues.

Taurus Negative Traits

Materialistic

The Taurus likes to live the good life. Although the Taurus will try to keep up frugal financial appearances, don't let the bull fool you—the credit card statements are just hidden well. They do, however, figure out the finances. Although the Taurus is smart enough to know that they can't take their possessions with them to the grave, they will hoard as much as they can to try to fulfill something emotionally missing in their life. They want the best of the best, and they don't care if there's a coupon or discount or not.

Lazy

With the Taurus and their intellect and motivated drive, a negative of being lazy sounds like an oxymoron. However, the Taurus can be incredibly lazy unless it benefits them or is interesting to them. You will know when a Taurus isn't stimulated because they are good at ignoring and going into idle mode.

Argumentative

When things don't go well for the go-getter Taurus, they quickly become frustrated and short-tempered. The bull festers and then everything frustrating about the now, the past, and the possible future heats up the emotions and an argument is sure to ensue. You might say black, they will say white. When emotional, the Taurus rarely sees any gray area. The Taurus is a fixed sign, which means they fix themselves to their beliefs. It's hard to change their minds, and they will happily challenge your ideas, opinions, and arguments.

Taurus Keywords

possessive
DEPENDABLE
REALISTIC
self-indulgent
materialistic
determined
PREDICTABLE

Taurus Communication Style

The Taurus isn't a small talker, but that doesn't mean they aren't communicators. They believe actions speak loudly, and they don't want to waste their time or breath on small talk, useless conversation, or superficial relationships. To capture the attention of a Taurus, do it over a scrumptious dinner, or next to a comfortable fire, and make sure the communication is lively. Soon enough the Taurus will open up. They are amazing listeners and will remember something you told them years ago, so be careful what you say.

Taurus Misconceptions

Only Wants the Finer Things

Yes, the Taurus likes their things, but the stereotype that everything they want is flashy, fast, and fun is often a major misconception. Ask a Taurus what matters most and it won't be their bling or the sport's car, it will be their friends and family.

Don't Be a Taurus, Taurus

Taurus, you don't like to be wrong—we get it. The thing is, sometimes you are and then you cover it with lies and manipulation. You are loved for being so solid and grounded, but not so much for the "it's my way or no way" attitude. Notorious for being stubborn, your lesson is that compromise isn't losing and that everyone is wrong sometimes. Yes, even you, Taurus.

Thoughts from a Taurus

The Ambivert

Many Taurean energies are ambiverts, meaning they are very social, but on a dime, they decide not to be and would rather call in for pizza and play on their laptop. You may have plans canceled often with a Taurus, but don't ask them to explain themselves as that will just push them away.

> "Being a Taurus is like being a combination of completely loyal, trustworthy, reliable, honest, compassionate, empathetic, and giving, with a touch of rage if you take me for granted! This is a challenge to overcome and learn to handle things in a different, positive way. By using the positive traits, I've also learned how to voice my feelings and stand up for myself when walked on. It creates a nice balance effect and a more peaceful lifestyle. I'll give you everything but don't pull me by my horns!"
> —Alexandria

Creative

They have been known to love things gaudy and loud, but it is true that Taureans are creative and have eclectic taste. A Taurean needs to live with beauty around them. This isn't always materialistic, though; it's a calming, beautiful energy that can also mean a happy home or the company they keep.

> "I'm a lover of all things beautiful, from art and jewelry, nature, to being comfortable yet practical in my home. I am very compassionate about all living things even down to spiders who terrify me, which is probably why I'm a natural-born vegetarian. I'm an artist and writer at heart with a love for taking photos of whatever catches my eye."
> —Cat

Emotional

A Taurus energy is most known for their hard-headed, stubborn-like qualities, but emotional isn't a quality that you typically hear when describing "the bull." The stubbornness is often because they want everything perfect, not for just themselves but for the ones they love.

> "Over the years, I've come to embrace being a male Taurus. Most people think because we are 'hard-headed' that real emotion doesn't exist in our realm. It's quite the contrary. I think that most Taurus men, myself included, have an emotional side/soft spot that we try to hide because we don't want to seem or feel less masculine. When I'm sad, I tend to bottle up those emotions, so as not to 'bother' those around me. It's not an easy feat for me to be open about my emotions, but when I feel comfortable enough with someone, it tends to not be an issue. When it comes to friendships, I am one of the most loyal people you could meet and would do anything for the people I love. As far as relationships, although we don't always show much emotion, we have a very romantic side and will do anything to show love and affection to whomever we are pursuing or whomever we are involved with. I see my Taurus side often, including being stubborn, but at the same time I am extremely reliable and responsible and always willing to take on new challenges."
>
> —Evan

Taurus and Relationships

Strengths

A Taurus is reliable, loyal, and somewhat predictable. Those who need a bit more pizzazz in a relationship may consider the Taurus dull. Taureans are homebodies, but they do love a night out once in a while. They can pretty much make themselves content in any environment. The dependability and surprisingly romantic energy of a Taurus makes for a sweet relationship. They love intellectual conversations.

Taurus energies love things that smell good, taste good, feel good, and sound good. They are simpler than they try to present themselves to be.

Challenges

Taurus energies need a degree of patience. They take everything very slowly, including romantic relationships and friendships. Trust must be earned. Taurus energies don't love to partake in serious discussions unless they initiate it. If you attempt to second-guess their decisions or counsel them on their past, they will shut down. The more you push, the harder it is to win that emotional trust back.

Taurus in the Workplace

Strengths

Your Taurus boss is hard-working, dependable, and calm. They do well with those who are self-starters and those who don't need to be micromanaged, as they put a lot on their own plate and don't have time to babysit their staff. If, by chance, there is someone who needs extra energy, you will see the Taurus anxiety and grumpiness come out. They like meetings and make sure everyone is on common ground.

A Taurus boss will tell you what they need and how they need it. They are likely to share their own successes with others who have helped along the path.

Challenges

Taurus bosses have a hard time dealing with others who try to backstab or undermine them. They don't love exaggerated personalities and instead do better with someone who likes routine and order like they do. If the Taurus isn't happy, you will likely get the cold shoulder.

Parenting a Taurus Child

Your little Taurean is relentless. They will do whatever it is to tire their parents down so that they give in and the child can get their way. It's important to set rules, regulations, and teach the Taurean child proper boundaries.

Strengths

Happy: The Taurus child is typically very happy, caring, affectionate, loyal, loving, and needs love.

Emotionally Stable: One of the most stable of all zodiacs, the Taurus child is pretty easy to understand; they just need a routine and consistency that works for everyone.

Earthy: The Taurus child isn't afraid to get their hands dirty or their feet in the ocean water. They love to be outside exploring.

Musical: Hand your Taurus child a musical instrument, a pot and spoon, or turn up the music and you'll see your Taurus flourish.

Dedicated: Taurus children are very loving and loyal. They are dedicated to those who love them.

Challenges

Lazy: Taurus children are often seen as lazy, but although they may not always be physically inclined, they are continually exercising intellectually. The Taurus child does not like to be pushed to do anything and will stand their ground, digging in their heels, which can cause a lot of frustration.

Temper: Just know that the temper tantrums are fierce, and you will likely see that play out more times than you'd like to. And they are stubborn; the more you push, the more they push back.

Needs Routine: Taurus children need routine and consistency. You will see the stubbornness of the Taurus when they have a parent who is unorganized or spontaneous.

Overly Confident: Despite the typical stereotype of being strong-willed, Taurus children are so much smarter than what they believe. They pretend to have high self-esteem, but they often second-guess themselves.

Taurus as a Parent

Strengths

Stability: A Taurus parent wants stability for their child and offers consistency with doses of fun.

Confidence: They rarely talk down to their child and instead want to instill confidence and independence for their child, trying to encourage and love.

Nature-loving: The Taurus parent tends to love nature and the outdoors and wants to give their child the same experiences, whether hiking or gardening.

Traditional: A Taurus parent tends to be quite traditional, whether with holiday traditions or bedtime traditions.

Balanced: Kind and compassionate, a Taurus parent is very grounded. They love to have fun, all the while showing that hard work and fun have to be balanced. The Taurus parent is nurturing and giving, trying to fulfill their child's needs.

Challenges

Lack of Flexibility: The Taurus parent requires constant flexibility. They can be preoccupied with whatever is going on in their life and the child can sometimes feel like they are in the way.

Pushover: They are softies who can be pushovers. They might say "no," but it doesn't take much to flip them into a "yes."

Distracted: The Taurus parent is often distracted by whatever is on their schedule and can become forgetful of what the priority is—their child. This is why routine and a schedule are important.

Taurus and Finances

Taurus energies are practical, sometimes thought of as frugal or tight. They create financial spreadsheets and make pro/con lists of, well, everything. The Taurus handles their finances in a rational and predicable fashion. For a spouse of a Taurus it may feel controlling.

Moon in Taurus

Taurus energy is all about hard work and reliability. This energy takes work, financial situations, and life very seriously and puts a lot of pressure on themselves.

New Moon in Taurus

When the moon moves into Taurus you might feel exhausted, tired, moody, and even just plain sick and depleted. The mood swings like a possessed pendulum. If possible, during this time get takeout, light a yummy-smelling candle, watch television, or read that book you keep meaning to pick up, and call it an early night. Caring for all your senses helps you get through this phase.

The New Moon in Taurus makes it a wonderful time to begin a new career and look over money/finances. A Taurus is a hard worker and a reliable employee. They take work, financial situations, and life very seriously, and put a lot of pressure on themselves. They like the nicer things in life and will make the extra effort to make sure to afford that. Often practical and pragmatic (sometimes to a fault), Taurus don't play well with stupid people or those who lack common sense. And Taurus especially has a lack of tolerance around those who don't pull their weight. So even though you might not be a Taurus, you embrace the energy of the sign and in turn take on aspects of that sign. So, those who aren't pulling their weight in your life (romantically, family, or work), be cautious of what you say. It's easy to channel the Taurus's pig-headedness and angry outbursts, which can push people away and stir up drama. With regard to romance, jealousy and possessiveness will be the name of the game during this time. You might just want to bite your tongue and let the energy blow over.

This moon encourages a sense of self-worth and allows for exploration of inspiration. Taurus, being an earth sign, isn't always thrilled with the idea of embracing the sensitive side, but when the New Moon visits Taurus, it offers an intuitive nudge and uncovers sensible creativity. A Taurus often puts up roadblocks they themselves construct as a means for self-sabotage. The New Moon energy activates the idea that it's okay to dig deep and simply stop and smell the roses.

What You May See during the New Moon Phase of Taurus:

> The ability to be patient with others and, most importantly, with oneself.
>
> Inspirational ideas for career and financial earnings.
>
> The motivation to make everyone around you comfortable and content.
>
> The freedom to indulge.
>
> The realization that the journey doesn't always have to be stressful.

Full Moon in Taurus

Energy a few days beforehand and a few days after a Full Moon tends to be unstable. It can affect you and others emotionally and sometimes even physically.

Weather disasters and natural disasters are quite common during this time, so don't be surprised when you see some heavy news.

Taurus energy has the worst time coping with feeling manipulated/taken advantage of, being financially unstable, and loving hard and failing. Be careful during this time that your stubbornness doesn't take over. You might just want to bite your tongue and let the energy blow over. During this moon phase, you might feel sluggish and have a hard time concentrating or thinking clearly.

Soul Work

Write down ten things that you want to stop in your life and then rip up or burn the list; then write down ten things that you do want in your life and focus on those!

Now Is the Time

Do feel the anger and express it, even just writing it down and throwing it out. Don't point fingers and blame everybody and anybody. Do speak up. Don't stay quiet. Do take action in all aspects of your life. Don't just sit and wait for someone to do this and that for you. It won't happen. Do make decisions and follow through on them. This is not the time to be passive. Don't delay decisions. Do practice being brave and courageous, even with little things. Don't run away from the shadows.

Taurus Totem Animal

Sea Serpent

The sea serpent is mystical and magical. Mess with this energy and they may very well lash out. Just as the sea serpent's counterpart, the snake, sheds its skin, the sea serpent also hides behind his illusions. The sea serpent deserves respect. They want to always create, transform, and slither or swim away before they are figured out. The Taurus energy needs to trust the intuition to trust the process.

The sea serpent offers a gift of:

Power

Mysticism

Business success

Influence

Creativity

Charm

three
GEMINI
May 21–June 21
Air Energy ♊

Gemini is the third sign in the zodiac and is represented by the twins. Gemini is a mutable energy, meaning that it is ever changeable. As much as Geminis often fight the stereotype of being "the twins," many recognize that they can embrace the Jekyll and Hyde energy, especially when the emotions are heightened.

The Gemini is the communicator and always knows what to say, when to say it, and exactly how to say it. Geminis are social butterflies and often need company, even if it's chatting on the computer with a stranger—because before that conversation is over that stranger will be their best friend and vice versa. Geminis simply need to have the company of another.

The energy of the Gemini may very well feel emotionally stormy, and they can be their own worst enemy; but don't you dare call them out on the rain cloud above their head or else you'll see what their storm clouds can unleash.

Geminis are often insomniacs, with the ever-creative mind thinking and plotting. Gems will often express their exhaustion of body, mind, and soul. That creativity can be stifled under the light of day when action can be taken. Instead, they stay busy helping others with their dramas, picking up the shards of glass of their kept company, making sure that everything is perfect for others and often forgetting about themselves.

The dualistic energy can be adventurous. One minute they're fine and, just like that, anger or sadness erupts. Gemini energies pretend to be hard-to-figure-out people, but they are anything but complex; they just crave simple harmony. They want good music, creative projects, people to do what they say they are going to do, yummy food, and some peace and quiet when they say so.

Gemini Decans

Each zodiac is broken down into triplicities, each having their own energy added to their zodiac sign. This is Gemini broken down:

Gemini of First Decan: May 22–31
Ruled by Mercury.

Positive Energy Traits: This Gemini is the observer and seeker. Often distracted, but always available for fun conversation, they would take their shirt off to help a stranger. They are fast talkers and quick thinkers, knowing exactly how to execute and organize, and will often give others all the credit.

Negative Energy Traits: Can be "on" for others, but deep inside there's a lot of sadness from childhood. They may detach themselves without communicating the whole story. The biggest mistake the Gem can make is to assume others will believe in them. The journey never looks identical to someone else's. Because everyone's journey is different, there will be some who will never understand the Gem journey. That's okay, they don't have to understand the journey. But when the Gemini gets to where they are going on the transformation, there will be no denying that the journey was worth it. Often this Gemini's mind is racing ahead during conversations and they can be accused of not paying attention or of being unfocused.

Gemini of Second Decan: June 1–10
Ruled by Venus.

Positive Energy Traits: They love all things beautiful and seek the same for themselves but also seek to share with those they love. This Gemini is a wonderful conversationalist—able to heal with words. They are the psychologists and social workers of friends and family. This Gemini is a hopeless romantic and will seek out a better world for themselves and those they love. Always available to lend an ear or a shoulder to cry on, this energy is a feeler and a doer, always willing to help with solutions.

Negative Energy Traits: This Gemini can be restless and lose focus as they overanalyze. This energy is the epitome of being their own worst enemy. Indecisiveness for this Gemini is one of the biggest Achilles heels. Others see it as being unreliable. This Gemini often needs to learn to believe in themselves and that it's okay to self-care and to climb whatever ladder they build. If this Gemini thinks that you've betrayed them, you will be met with both twins: cold and resentful. This energy expects a lot of themselves, but also of those around them.

Gemini of Third Decan: June 11–21
Ruled by Uranus.

Positive Energy Traits: This Gemini is the humanitarian who has big ideas, is social, and has a contagious, friendly attitude. They love to learn and continually seek their personal vision, not to benefit themselves but to help share a wealth of knowledge. This Gemini is adventurous and whimsically rebellious. This energy is blunt and straightforward, which can be both a positive and a negative. If you wonder if your rear end looks big in your new jeans, you will likely be told the truth by this Gemini. While some people may think they are mean, they're simply giving you sincere honesty.

Negative Energy Traits: This Gemini can be detached and moody. Although they may have a lot of ideas, they don't always have a lot of energy to follow through. This Gem will complain about the same thing, although they have the solution, just no follow-through. They are continually seeking their personal vision but want others to do the work to make it so.

May Gemini vs. June Gemini

Along with each sign being split into their third decans, there is a difference between each zodiac split between the months.

The May Gemini is calm, cool, and collected.

The June Gemini is outspoken and direct.

The May Gemini is spontaneous.

The June Gemini is a worrier.

The May Gemini is charming.

The June Gemini gets bored easily.

The May Gemini is often impulsive with finances.

The June Gemini is always concerned with finances.

The May Gemini will make changes if needed.

The June Gemini will wonder why changes aren't happening.

Gemini Masculine and Feminine Energy

Energy has a yin and yang that is interpreted as feminine and masculine, and according to the energy it is explained below:

Feminine May Gemini: The feminine energy of a Gemini in May is bubbly and wise beyond their years. This Gem is intuitive and a natural leader. They are loyal and honest. They require a circle filled with a like-minded and joy-filled tribe.

Masculine May Gemini: The masculine energy of a Gemini in May is positive and adventurous. They love to be on the move, always thinking of new ways to improve their life. This Gem can be unreliable and spontaneous. They are afraid of divulging their needs and wants, and shut down, ghosting those they love, appearing uncaring.

Feminine June Gemini: The feminine Gemini energy in June is witty, creative, and fun to be with. This Gem likely excels at painting, pottery, gardening, flower arranging, writing, cooking, photography—you name it. If they don't know how to do it, they'll figure it out. Geminis are social creatures; they love to chit and they love to chat. There is a dark side to the June Gemini: They are super sensitive and try to make everything look so perfect, always multitasking, and afraid to practice their "no," until they exhaust themselves into depression, anger, and resentment.

Masculine June Gemini: This Gemini masculine energy in June is like a complicated mathematical problem. They don't want to be figured out and challenge those who try. They are moody and can be their own worst enemies, even on a good day. They're afraid of their checkbook balance and concerned at the longevity of their jobs—something that consumes their thoughts. This Gem does love the creative world and needs music to help soothe their soul.

Gemini Positive Traits

Clever

Don't ever underestimate the *intelligence* of a Gemini. Gems are clever in many aspects, from figuring out sticky situations for a friend to finding solutions in the corporate world to YouTubing how to make the perfect Christmas bows. The more the Gemini must figure out, the happier they are.

Advisors

Because Geminis are intelligent and good listeners, they are always willing to lend an ear and offer pragmatic advice. Geminis are intuitive and have a keen ability to problem solve for their friends, family, and even strangers. It is valued advice, as they see all sides with reason and logic.

Friendly

There is no stranger in the world of a Gemini. Typically very happy-go-lucky, the Gem loves to socialize with a variety of people and will rarely find their place in just one clique; they're often accepted in several different tribes.

Gemini Negative Traits

Gossiper

The Gemini is the messenger and they take that responsibility seriously, which sometimes equates to telling others' secrets and stirring the pot. Some may find the gossiping Gemini as two-faced or manipulative, and tire of their continued "poking the bear." A Gemini feels it's their job to spread the word of whatever they feel the word should be.

Inconsistent

The Gemini changes their mind a lot, mostly because of new information and updated beliefs and principles, and not necessarily because of stubbornness. The Gemini energy is constantly thinking and trying to look at everything from different perspectives in order to broaden their mind.

Anxious

Gemini is full of energy but tends to bite off more than they can chew. Their long list of projects leads to anxiousness and emotional outbursts. The Gemini can be so frustrated and yet they don't know how to delegate their "to do" list to get things done quicker. Sometimes it's because of control, and other times it's because they don't want to ask for assistance.

Gemini Keywords

Gemini Communication Style

You will know a Gemini because they are the one hyperactively talking to anyone who will talk to them with curiosity. The Gemini truly loves to talk, and conversations are most often filled with ideas and creative thinking. This energy would rather you discuss with them in a verbal way than assume or send cryptic texts or emails.

Gemini Misconceptions

Geminis are often considered flighty and naïve, but the Gemini is intelligent, curious, and the seeker of information. Although they have high energy with a constant adjustable attitude, they are ever-changing, which makes them more complex. This sometimes is seen as being gullible, which is a misconception.

Don't Be a Gemini, Gemini

Gem? Gemini? Gem Gem? GEMINI?! You are so busy chatting away you aren't even listening! It's not because you don't care about others; it's your Gemini superpower of enthusiasm. You are social, yes, and gossipy, oh yeah, but watch that the conversation is a two-way street. There are times you believe your problems and your celebrations are the most important, and that can turn off your friends and family. We won't even get into the wishy-washy indecisiveness—you often ask, "do I want that or this, or this or that?" and when you get advice you do absolutely nothing with this or that. The lesson for you, Gem, is that fickleness is part of your makeup, but be careful of playing the victim.

Thoughts from a Gemini

Worry-Wart

"There are days when as a Gemini I can be chatty, always thinking, but sometimes that turns to worry. As a Gemini I want to be in control of my hobbies, family/friend situations, personal life, and work and have a feeling of all that's going on. My weakness, I've experienced, can be my lack of confidence while reviewing the past, which can be blinding. I also talk way too much. My babbling, though, makes me feel like I'm getting closer to achieving my desires. An oddity about being a Gemini is I get mass anxiety alone around lots of people, especially new people; making the love life difficult. Success in my career as a Gemini has always been involved in the front line, providing customer service or satisfaction."

—Ryan

May the Odds Be in Your Favor

Geminis thrive on not being figured out. The sweet and innocent personality is very true, but so is the moody and standoffish personality.

"They say Geminis have a dual personality, and for me that is true in so many ways. One thing is for sure, I have worked retail since 1981 and I have a different customer service voice versus my regular talking voice, and the dual personality spills over into everything in my life. My two favorite movies are *Jaws* and *The Sound of Music*; you cannot get more polar opposite than those. I am also an artist and I tend to analyze and overthink things, so I really have that left/right brain thing going on. I live by lists, but I long to just let it all go and wing it. Being a Gemini is a little confusing to people who know me. I'm happy and laughing one minute, and then crying about something the next, which is not unusual. And crying could be because of something as simple as a Hallmark movie, or something way more serious. With Geminis you just never know! All in all, I love being a Gemini, as we are a fun bunch. As for the ability for our moods to change in the snap of a finger, may the odds be ever in your favor!"

—Mary

Ever Changing

Don't think that you've figured out the Gemini, because just when you think you have, they pivot.

"I am the quintessential Gemini. Lively, talkative, interested, and interesting: I can talk to anyone on just about anything. I'm curious about the world, both natural and man-made. Gregarious and charming, I want to know about you and at the same token can often (and easily) sell you on ideas or products you may never have before considered. But beware, I can just as easily become bored and need to move on to a different stimulus. Sometimes, I can seem closed, aloof, and self-centered, too. But that side of my personality never lasts long, because I need the positive energy I receive from my engaging interactions with you!"

—Jennifer

Gemini and Relationships

Strengths

Gemini, an air sign, needs a relationship that is continually moving with constant stimulation and fun energy. One moment they want to ride the roller coaster, the next they hate the roller coaster and love the tilt-a-whirl. Their strength is the spontaneous nature. Those that like life more streamlined will find this a challenge.

Challenges

When crossed, Geminis have a quick wit and a sharp tongue. They are a wild creature that doesn't want to be corralled into one place. They are flirty, and this can cause problems for relationships that aren't stable. They often look for the worst to happen without any indication that anything bad is on the horizon.

Gemini in the Workplace

Strengths

A Gemini boss is friendly and social, thriving on communication from all those they work with and around. They are an active manager, wanting to know how you are doing and feeling, and will want regular updates on both your work and your personal life. They work well with others who embrace spontaneity and are turn-on-the-dime personalities. They can improvise and think on their feet and need their team to do the same.

Challenges

Gemini bosses can often get distracted and not delegate work appropriately. While appearing cool and calm, they can be moody and nervous, often feeling overwhelmed and worried.

Parenting a Gemini Child

Your Gemini child needs mental stimulation and needs to be kept busy with things to learn and things to do. This keeps the Gem from misbehaving. Let them express themselves and teach them to communicate, but also to listen to what others say to them.

Strengths

Social: A Gemini child is overall very happy, loves to laugh, and is social. Sign your child up for playgroups and activities and watch your child blossom.

Wanderers: Often seen as flighty, they aren't at all—they are the wanderers and the wonderers, ever-curious.

Chatty: Your Gemini child loves to chit-chat and socialize with anyone who might want to listen to them. Offer them an opportunity to learn a foreign language and they will likely flourish.

Smart: The Gemini is awfully smart but stays humble, not flaunting their intelligence. They like to stay curious and engaged.

Challenges

Needs Entertaining: Gemini kids need a lot of attention and a lot of entertainment, especially if they are an only child.

A Handful: Gemini children can be a handful, and that only increases the older they get. The Gemini child needs a serene environment and to be handled in the calmest manner possible.

Exaggerators: You sometimes have to take what your Gem says with a grain of salt since they are good at dramatizing the good and the bad—often seen as white lies and fibs.

Curious: Geminis are always curious and love to investigate to find answers, which is both a strength and a challenge. They will be the child that finds Santa's hidden Christmas presents or the one eavesdropping on parents' conversations. The twin personality can come out and might be interpreted as sneaky and manipulative.

Gemini as a Parent

Strengths

Adventurer: A Gemini parent likes to be on the go: exploring, traveling, and socializing. Whether it's a summer camping trip or camping in the living room, the Gemini parent can make anything an adventure.

Participator: Considered the fun parent, the Gemini energy loves to talk and participate in all their child's activities. They are the one signing up to help bake cookies for the Cookie Walk, volunteering at the class trip, and running for PTA president.

Creative: Need help with a science project? The Gemini parent will help. Need a family ancestry? Yup, the Gem parent will figure it out. Or if you need five dozen cookies for the bake sale or sequins sewn onto a dance costume, it's the Gemini parent who will assist.

Encourager: The one huge strength about a Gemini parent is that they are wonderful encouragers. Even if they don't always encourage themselves, they are there to pick up their child and support them through to the finish line.

Challenges

Chit and Chat: The Gemini parent may be so busy talking to their child that they forget to listen.

Friend Not Parent: They may be so busy trying to be the child's friend that they forget or shirk responsibility of being a parent.

Mood Swings: If life isn't running as smoothly as the Gemini energy believes it should, then their mood swings and everybody in their life pays for it.

Victimize: Sometimes considered emotionally wishy-washy, they can victimize themselves and delve into a deep depression, allowing their child to have to parent themselves and even parent the parent.

Gemini and Finances

The Gemini energy tends to get distracted and overwhelmed. They are smart and know how to handle finances with wisdom and resourcefulness. The twin in the Gemini, however, can overspend and then have buyer's remorse the next moment. The financial portfolio of a Gemini often looks more dizzying than a Ferris wheel.

Moon in Gemini

Because Gemini rules communication, you might be overanalyzing or feeling as if someone or something is out to get you. Be careful of misjudging scenarios at this time, and instead set your intentions on what you want and not what you don't want. The dualistic energy can make someone who is decisive and practical feel as if they are going crazy.

New Moon in Gemini

When the moon moves into Gemini energy you may very well feel emotionally stormy and that you are your own worst enemy. And sleep? Yeah, there's not much of that. You will likely feel exhausted from all the brain tabs open with endless lists.

Because Gemini rules communication, you might be overanalyzing or feeling as if someone or something is out to get you. Be careful of misjudging scenarios at this time, and instead set your intentions on what you want.

What You May See during the New Moon Phase of Gemini:

Bullying yourself.

Trusting others more than yourself.

Anxiety. Anxiety. More anxiety.

Unrealistic demands on yourself.

Wanting someone to save you.

Feeling like a failure.

Giving up and accepting failure.

Waiting for the motivation to get going.

Full Moon in Gemini

Feeling sad? Ornery? Like your mind won't shut off? You very well will feel the dualistic energy. Gemini energy never disappoints as it's always an adventure dealing with the energy of the twins. One minute you (or another) will be just fine and just like that, anger or sadness erupts. The bipolar personality of this moon makes it hard to figure people out (even those closest to you), and sometimes even yourself during this time. You will more than likely encounter a lot of grumpy people and a lot of erratic drivers. The positive with this moon (there is always a positive and negative), is that this is a great time to embrace your spirituality, take a fun class, express your love, and treat life with as much simplicity as you can. Gemini moons are not complex, they just crave simple harmony. Turn your music on loud, start a creative project (or finish one), and be careful of over-complicating things. If you do you will see the Jekyll & Hyde personality come out in yourself and those around you. The Full Moon will bring a lot of self-discovery, so be careful what you wish for.

Soul Work

Stop the "Yeah but …" Are you saying any of the following statements? Yeah but I don't have enough money. Yeah but I will never have enough money. Yeah but it's impossible. Yeah but what would my family say? Yeah but it's too hard. Yeah but I don't have enough time. Yeah but I should just be thankful for what I have. Yeah but what if someone gets mad at me. Yeah but I'm scared.

Replace the statements with these affirmations: Yeah, I have enough money. Yeah, it's possible. Yeah, family might talk, but so what? Yeah, it's hard but I'm worth it. Yeah, I have enough time. Yeah, I should be thankful for what I have, and I'm allowed to have more. Yeah, someone might get mad at me, but it's because they are afraid. Yeah, I'm scared, but the more I work on this the more confident I'll become. **You can *Yeah* all you want; stop the *but*.**

Now Is the Time

Do look at ways to create new in your life. Don't make excuses for why you can't take steps forward. Do communicate your feelings and ideas with family and friends. Don't get upset if they don't communicate the way you do. Do finish a project, sign up for school, or a class you've been wanting to take. Don't beat yourself up over not finishing the project or knowing everything that you wish you already knew.

Gemini Totem Animal

Fox

It's no surprise that the totem animal of the Gemini is the fox. The fox energy is cunning but has a soft side. They don't love to show their true selves to just anyone. Instead, they might act as the center of attention, all the while cracking jokes with a wicked sense of humor. The Gemini energy is zestful, creative, and sexy even without trying. The fox is energetic and witty.

The fox offers a gift of:

Cleverness

Trickster

Protectiveness

Sexiness

Tenderheartedness

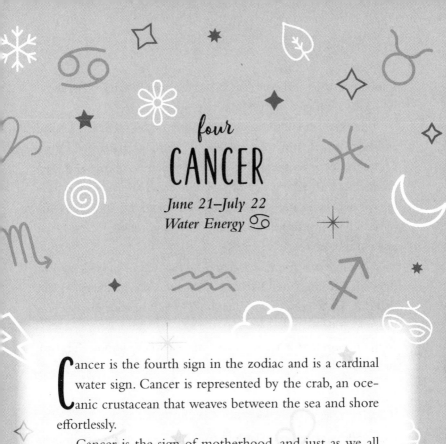

four
CANCER
June 21–July 22
Water Energy ♋

Cancer is the fourth sign in the zodiac and is a cardinal water sign. Cancer is represented by the crab, an oceanic crustacean that weaves between the sea and shore effortlessly.

Cancer is the sign of motherhood, and just as we all have a different experience with our mothers, that energy is interpreted differently for each Cancer. Some fight the origin of their astrological sign by trying to be cold, hard, and unfeeling like the shell they carry. Others feel the need to be the keeper of hearth and home, readily revealing their compassionate and gentle nature. Cancer is emotionally powerful and highly intuitive.

The Cancer is attached to family life, whether it be biological family or friends that they consider their family. The Cancer energy is a hopeless romantic and looks for kindness in everyone and everything. Some see this as overly sensitive,

sometimes naïve, and even fragile, and they can be targeted by those who take advantage of the Cancer's positive nature.

Since Cancer is a water sign, the water makes them feel relaxed and helps them clear the cobwebs of the mind. It's so hard for a Cancer to focus on themselves as they are compassionate and keep themselves busy taking care of everyone else. This can lead to feeling overwhelmed and stressed, and guilty for taking time for themselves. They love to feel *needed* and thrive on caring for everyone else but themselves.

Although easygoing and giving, be careful not to walk all over the crab, because you'll likely be met with their pinchers. It's not that they are keeping track, but you'll be put in your place if you overstep your boundaries.

It's important for a Cancer to continue to grow, move forward, and know that risks aren't always reckless.

Cancer Decans

Each zodiac is broken down into triplicities, each having their own energy added to their zodiac sign. This is Cancer broken down:

Cancer of First Decan: June 22–July 1
Ruled by the Moon.

Positive Energy Traits: This Cancer is caring and compassionate, authentic and sensitive. Their heart is filled with kindness, and they have an uncanny way of understanding from the perspective of others and acting accordingly. This Cancer is the one who will stay with her best friend's grandma in the hospital even though they've only met her once. Cancer will drive hundreds of miles if you call and say you are stranded.

Negative Energy Traits: This Cancer is a worrier. They worry what others might think about them. They worry that someone is going to hurt them, and they wonder how. They are consumed with concern that they aren't doing everything they should be doing and how that might be perceived by others. They think so much and create monsters where there are none, sometimes manifesting trouble so they don't look neurotic.

Cancer of Second Decan: July 2–12
Ruled by Pluto.

Positive Energy Traits: This Cancer is loving and has great instincts, especially with helping others. They are balanced and grounded, making others attracted to their wisdom and advice. This Cancer values friendships and will drop everything to lend their support to someone going through a rough patch. It is their intuitiveness that makes them a special force and a pillar to their friends and family.

Negative Energy Traits: This Cancer needs to be needed and if you don't call on them for their advice or assistance you will face a sad and overly sensitive soul. They can become unreasonable with jealousies and sometimes come across as unapproachable. They want to dig for answers and can back people into a corner looking for information that may or may not be the truth, turning off people they love.

Cancer of Third Decan: July 13–22
Ruled by Neptune.

Positive Energy Traits: This Cancer is very sensitive and incredibly intuitive. They are the epitome of a nurturer. This Cancer is the encourager and is gifted with an empath nature, which is often carried over to them being the therapist to their friends and family. They are amazing at keeping secrets, giving loving but sensible advice. The undying loyalty and generosity of this Cancer make them a gift to all who call them a friend or family member.

Negative Energy Traits: As much as this Cancer is an amazing friend, if you take advantage of that loyalty you will be met by someone who isn't afraid to slam the door shut without any opportunity to apologize. Forgiveness doesn't come easily for this decan, and their suspicious nature can crash the trust as quickly as it was built. This Cancer can be moody and have a mess of doubts when it comes to their own life: They need reassurance and a lot of communication. Healers often don't understand how to heal themselves, and this Cancer knows this all too well.

June Cancer vs. July Cancer

Along with each sign being split into their third decans, there is a difference between each zodiac split between the months.

June Cancer craves security.

July Cancer is private.

June Cancer likes to be nurtured.

July Cancer likes to nurture.

June Cancer is creative.

July Cancer is intuitive.

June Cancer gets frustrated easily.

July Cancer gets jealous easily.

Cancer Masculine and Feminine Energy

Energy has a yin and yang that is interpreted as feminine and masculine, and according to the energy it is explained below:

Feminine June Cancer: The feminine energy of a Cancer in June is confident, intelligent, and determined. They may pretend to be tough and guarded to save face, but they are very compassionate and nurturing. Once you earn their trust you will have a forever friend. If you mess up that trust, out you go.

Masculine June Cancer: The masculine energy of a Cancer in June was born to be a leader. They are career-oriented and strong-willed. They display amazing understanding and a sixth sense in the boardroom or bedroom.

Feminine July Cancer: The feminine energy of a Cancer in July was born to people-please; they are sensitive, and are emotional caregivers. They love creativity, embracing their intuition, and nurturing others. Although a huge flirt, Cancer is loyal. Wildly independent, they do love to be part of a social circle and be the main listener; but they don't tell their own secrets. Sometimes they can come across as clingy and needing reassurance.

Masculine July Cancer: The masculine energy of July Cancer is sweet and loving, genuinely interested in the ones they love and what is going on in their lives. They can seem needy and insecure, sometimes looking dull and boring because they are so routine and consistent. They are protective, and that can come across as jealous and tenacious.

Cancer Positive Traits

Loyal

The Cancer energy is incredibly loyal to everyone they meet. Once you befriend a Cancer you have a forever friend who is one of the most accepting and dependable of all the zodiacs. Although the Cancer energy can be moody, they are stable and consistent, even with their mood swings. They will communicate their needs and withdraw if they feel their energy isn't helpful. Their transparency is refreshing. The Cancer will do whatever it takes to put you first, never meaning to take you for granted. Cancers are easily loved because of their never-ending loyalty.

Intuitive

The Cancer energy is one of the most intuitive of all the zodiac signs. Extremely good listeners with natural maternal instincts, they are open to the human connection. Like a true water sign, Cancer's intuition is a direct line to the other side. Those who were born under this sign have the ability to invoke the moon and communicate with the other side, making them highly intuitive and magical. Cancerians can read people for who they are: good, bad, malicious, and indifferent, and although they don't deny the intuition, they want to believe in good in a world of the opposite. Don't try to pull one over on a Cancer, though, because they forgive but they never forget.

Independent

Don't mistake a Cancer's loyalty for codependency. The Cancer is independent and more than sufficient when it comes to handling life. Although the Cancerian is there for everyone else, they have a difficult time opening up to others, afraid of the vulnerability. It is their hidden emotion that often makes them look even more independent than they already are. The Cancer energy is not afraid of moving across country, or even out of the country, without knowing a soul, and quickly finds a job and their community.

Cancer Negative Traits

Temperamental

Cancer energies are so busy taking care of everyone else that a burnout comes fast and often. Because they have a hard time asking for help, the frustration builds, and they want to throw in the towel instead of fighting for their needs and wants. They sometimes sabotage themselves in their relationships by thinking they are being positive, all the while being negative. They can either be super helpful and caring or aloof and nonchalant, and sometimes it's hard to tell which one they choose as their crab shell is hard to crack. They can be moody and irrational, retreating into their shells each and every time, until they feel it's safe to face the world again.

Possessive

Cancer energies are protective but can also become possessive. Cancer personalities feel the urge to make a mark on the world, all the while keeping family and friends who are close to their heart in the loop. Cancerians are happy to devote themselves entirely to the care and protection of their loved ones, striving hard to go above and beyond no matter what. There is, however, a fine line with Cancerians on this since their emotions always run deep. If the communication isn't clear, the stories in their head turn into jealousy and possessiveness.

Suspicious

Another trait that people should know about Cancers is that they are sensitive, which makes them open, and sometimes expecting to be hurt. It makes sense they have their shell to hide in. Even the suspicion of being hurt can run them into a passive space.

Cancer Keywords

Cancer Communication Style

Cancers are amazing listeners. The Cancer gives you all your attention with caring and compassion. You truly have a friend in a Cancer. A Cancer loves people who are vibrant and filled with energy and humor to offset the myriad of people who come to them with their problems. If you are having a bad day, the Cancer will be the first to offer a hug, a cup of a coffee, and a word of advice. If the Cancer is having a bad day, they will retreat and not communicate about their own feelings. Let them. Don't follow them into their shell but instead be there for them when they come out and are ready to face the world again—preferably with some humor and love.

Cancer Misconceptions

Don't ever underestimate a Cancerian's silence for ignorance. Their uncanny calmness isn't acceptance, and their forgiveness is not a weakness. It takes a lot for a Cancer to walk away from someone, and if you've been cut off, it's more than likely final.

Don't Be a Cancer, Cancer

Your mood faucet doesn't have a lukewarm setting; instead it's hot or it's cold. It's yes or it's no. You are known for putting walls up, Cancer. You push friends away. You push love interests away. It's not that you mean to, though; you just don't trust. You are moody. You are sensitive. You care a lot. Then that scares you and you pretend that you don't care and never did. Your lesson, Cancer, is that being vulnerable is okay, but be careful not to make it look like insecurity.

Thoughts from a Cancer

Walking Mood Ring

Cancer energy is extremely intuitive and affectionate, but interestingly, as much as they want to help others, they are hesitant to divulge too much about themselves. That can come across as aloof or shy, but then they can be the first one to help plan the party.

> "I can be a walking mood ring who is highly sensitive and emotional. Water is my element and I can be easily ruled by all things of the heart. We function best with love and harmony in the house. As children, a lot of us do not have the defenses to deal well with the outside world. We can be brooders, and when things do

not go our way, it is nothing for us to want to hide in our shells. We are known to be good with money and good with food; a picnic comes to mind after a long day of coming to the rescue of others. We are staunch protectors of our loved ones and ask little in return."

—Alexandria

Remember Self-Care

Because Cancer energies are often busy nurturing everyone else, they often forget about themselves.

"As a Cancer you get told that your family must always come first to make your world complete. What they won't or don't tell you is that if you don't also take time for yourself and the wild imagination that we have, it will more than likely either: 1. Put you in the funny farm; or 2. It will shut you down almost completely emotionally. Cancers are also viewed as homebodies. Not the case at all. I personally love to get out and enjoy life; especially in nature and around our closest friends. Do not assume that we won't fight, either; even though we are a water sign, we know it can be a common trait. While we won't always get physical, mentally we can be very destructive."

—Laura

Guarded

Cancer energies do not want to be figured out. They are complicated and can come across as cool, calm, and collected, but inside they are having a panic attack. That hard shell can be quite cold, which is a protective measure since they can be easily hurt.

"Being a Cancer is as much of an emotional roller coaster as you might think. My crustacean shell keeps me guarded. Very few know the emotional center that lies within. Although once I allow you to crack open that shell, you're stuck in my claws for life. Family is everything to me. At the drop of a hat I would be there for anyone in my small circle. Like the typical water sign I feel most at home at the beach or next to any body of water. At times my emotions tend to get the best of me. Thankfully, my tough shell is always there to retreat into. I wouldn't change being a Cancer for anything! Even on days when I want to just save the world. Cancers rule!"

—Rachael

Cancer and Relationships

Strengths

The Cancer energies are extremely sensitive. They love their family and friends, and truly do cherish their relationships. They are extremely loyal and sentimental. They love to be romanced and to romance in return.

Challenges

Cancer energies can be very passive, holding on to the resentments that can grow into dirty bitterness. They love things just so, and if you aren't a mind reader for what they want out of the relationship, they often withdraw into their shell and stay there because they feel everything, and their intuition is often super heightened.

Cancer in the Workplace

Strengths

A Cancer boss is warm and friendly. They are good listeners and are grateful for a team that does their job. A Cancer boss honestly believes in everyone being peers and doesn't like the idea of a structured corporate ladder.

Challenges

Cancer bosses want everything to be smooth, like a fine-oiled machine. They don't take to being underestimated, and if they find out that you've been disloyal, they won't hesitate to cut you off.

Be careful not to underestimate a Cancer boss. They may come across as low-key and low maintenance, all the while being high-strung and nervous.

Cancer and Finances

Cancer energies are moody spenders. Often known to be thrifty spenders, they rarely over-spend but attempt to balance their finances and overthink the purchases. They do, however, like to purchase things that make them feel better depending upon their current mood. They are also very generous and will buy for others to try to make them feel better through thoughtful gifts. Sometimes they try to buy friendship with gifts before they realize what they are doing.

Parenting a Cancer Child

The peace and security of the Cancer's home makes for a happy child. Your emotional support of your Cancer child is important. They need family time. Put your phone down when talking to your Cancer. Schedule game night. Sit down and color. It's not that they need to be entertained; it's that they need quality time.

Strengths

Nurturers: They are nurturers and in return need to be nurtured. They prosper in a warm and loving family setting, and although they don't need to be micromanaged, they like a parent who is in touch and truly interested in their daily life.

Sensitive: There are positives to the Cancer child being so sensitive and that is because pretty much a look is all the discipline that's needed. They learn their lesson fast and they want to please their parents and teachers. They blossom with straightforward logic rather than a spanking.

Family Loving: The Cancer child loves their family, especially their mama. They are comfortable with staying home, not needing outside activities to keep them happy.

Challenges

Moody: Cancer children can be very moody. Instead of expressing their emotions, they can shut down and be temperamental, depressed, and sad. Cancer children are great at pouting and shutting down no matter what the parent does to try to get them to express their feelings.

Clingy: Cancers are known for being attached to their parents at a young age, so it won't be surprising when dropping them off for the first day of school to see them clinging to their parent's leg.

Homebodies: The Cancer child is known to be a homebody. The Cancer child may be excited about the sleepover, but be prepared to be called right before midnight to come pick them up because they're homesick. Or they decide not to do an activity or attend the school dance or birthday party, instead wanting to just stay home. It's important to teach this energy early on about fulfilling commitments and showing them that going outside their comfort zone is fine and that home will always be there.

Cancer as a Parent

Strengths

Natural Nurturer: A Cancer energy loves their children, and loves being a parent. They are adaptable and flexible, making time for the kids and their activities. The Cancer parent is a natural nurturer and loves the uniqueness of each child and fosters that.

Family: Family is everything and the Cancer parent loves surrounding their kids with their definition of what family entails.

Sentimental: The Cancer parent is sentimental and will surely keep every picture and report card, and will probably even dry the dandelions their child picks for them.

Challenges

Overly Sensitive: The Cancer parent can be overly sensitive if life isn't going perfectly. The Cancer parent needs to have a fair amount of love and loyalty back from the people in their life. If that doesn't happen, then the emotional shutdown occurs. It's important to lean on family and friends when feeling stressed and not to stifle or shut down as the children may interpret that as something they've done wrong.

Smothering: The Cancer parent can be smothering, wanting to know every detail of what's going on in their child's life. The need for information sometimes goes above being parental, and sometimes it's just plain nosy.

Anxious: The Cancer parent is often so anxious about every aspect of their life that it can affect their ability to parent, and sometimes this oozes over into their child being their friend rather than their child.

Moon in Cancer

When we are in the energy of the Cancer, we often feel everything. Cancer rules motherhood and so you may feel very emotional during this time. If your mom has crossed over, there may be an aching to talk to her. Or if you are lucky to still have Mom here, you may be urged to call or spend time with her. Note that this energy isn't just for those born under the Cancer sign.

New Moon in Cancer

The Cancer moon is the time to step forward and move ahead. It's time to take flight. This energy in Cancer is great for starting new projects that involve the home and family.

What You May See during the New Moon Phase of Cancer:

Home projects.

Being honest with yourself and others with regard to your relationship.

Beginning new hobbies or an artistic study.

Starting a family.

Napping.

Exploring your ancestry.

Spending time with family.

Signing up for school.

Spending time around water.

Embracing the emotions you feel.

During the time of the Cancer moon be careful of unrealistic expectations and unresolved business that may be hiding your true path. We can overcome anything if we allow ourselves to get out of our own way.

Full Moon in Cancer

For those who are extra empathic, be prepared as this Full Moon in Cancer is filled with a lot of energy. It might make you panic, or it might motivate you. It might make you feel exhausted or exhilarated.

On the negative side you may feel sad one moment, happy the next. Calm and then anxious, all without warning. People may react erratically with more road rage and become crazy drivers. Full Moons often bring strange weather patterns, and big scandals. You may feel more intuitive, have more paranormal experiences, and feel more tuned in to other's lies.

Self-care during this time helps with staying grounded. Drink hot drinks. Write a letter to someone you are upset with or missing, and then burn it. Hug a tree (really). Eat a salad. Take a hot bath with Epsom salts. Exercise. Smudge yourself. Diffuse some essential oils (lavender, cedarwood, or rosemary can help). Go out with friends or family. *Spend some more time thinking of what you did and what you can do rather than what you didn't do or can't do.*

It's also the time to get your crystals out to recharge them. Choose a location that feels happy and is safe from kids and pets. It can be a front porch, a windowsill, or even the dash of your car.

Frustration and impatience, two typical reactions to Full Moons, are both negative attributes, which throw more negativity your way. Turn off the negative mental chat that is sabotaging the life you so deserve. How do you do that? The first thing is by acknowledging that you are doing it, and when a negative thought arises, tell yourself "STOP!" and replace the negative thought with a positive one. Or simply take some deep breathes. We can't always have a head full of sunshine, but little by little you will notice that your negative thoughts will start to dissipate. Think of it as mental scum and you are erasing it away with your happy thoughts. By simply turning down the volume of negative chatter, the things you have been wanting in your life will begin to show up—whatever you are dreaming of. Always remember that what you focus on expands and if it is negative, then that is what you will get.

Soul Work
Cancers have issues letting go of the past. Being deeply sensitive, they forgive, but they rarely forget. This is a great time to see the benefit of releasing the baggage. Make a list of what you need to let go of and how you benefit from holding on to it. Imagine what it feels like to let go. How does it feel?

Now Is the Time
Do tell the people in your life about your hurt feelings. Don't harbor regrets. Do plan something for yourself, independently. Don't sit around at home all the time when there's so much adventure to be had. Do say exactly what you mean. Don't assume that those close to you know what you need and want. Do trust your intuition. Don't be afraid to say yes or no.

Cancer Totem Animal

Horse

The horse energy calls out to the Cancer to embrace freedom in their life, but not to race too fast through their time with the ones they love. The horse totem is one of service and hospitality, but burnout can occur if you don't stop and graze once in a while. The horse is an amazing caregiver—supportive, a wonderful listener, and resourceful.

The horse offers a gift of:

Fertility

Service

Hospitality

Freedom

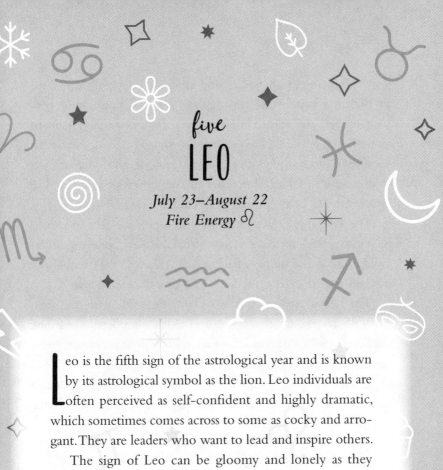

five
LEO

July 23–August 22
Fire Energy ♌

eo is the fifth sign of the astrological year and is known
by its astrological symbol as the lion. Leo individuals are
often perceived as self-confident and highly dramatic,
which sometimes comes across to some as cocky and arrogant. They are leaders who want to lead and inspire others.

The sign of Leo can be gloomy and lonely as they
feel the weight of the world on their shoulders. This often makes them reclusive. They have a loving heart and a
strong personality, but they are fragile, which creates that
perceived snobby misconception. Having to be the decision maker and pack leader is almost an unfair energy
that's been given to a Leo. The Leo desires affection and
approval, but their headstrong personality screams an *I'm
the one in charge* energy and that can void their softer side.

People who fall under the sign of the lion are fiercely
loyal and take it upon themselves to protect the underdogs,

devoting themselves to justice and kindness. They will work hard on their relationships, not shying away from responsibility in personal life and professional life, not afraid of carrying others' burdens and offering help and advice. They are honest and will expect the same from those around them—friend and foe alike. Appreciation is important to a Leo. They need to know they are loved, and in return you will be reciprocated with the lion's purr.

The Leo energy is caring; they are often the first to run to help someone. They have a high moral compass, believing in the Golden Rule and doing what is right. Although they will gladly help others, the Leo's pride has a hard time accepting help.

The Leo is creative, but has a hard time following through. They do great with ideas but not so much with details, and they get bored easily; they quickly move on to the next project, rarely finishing the previous.

The Leo doesn't want to be ignored, overlooked, or made to feel invisible. Do that once and they may let it slide but do it twice and you will likely hear them roar.

Leo Decans

Each zodiac is broken down into triplicities, each having their own energy added to their zodiac sign. This is Leo broken down:

Leo of First Decan: July 23–August 1
Ruled by the Sun.

Positive Energy Traits: Warm and self-reliant. This Leo is independent, extroverted, and gregarious in nature. They are flamboyant and have an outgoing personality that's hard to be ignored. You'll likely see them dancing in the middle of the grocery store, leading the charge in the board office, and motivating and encouraging their friends, coworkers, and family. It's rare to see this Leo sitting down for long. This Leo is a confident extrovert, although they like to come across as an introvert, who enjoys meeting and talking to new people. This Leo is loving and loyal. They love to adorn their friends and family with whatever might bring joy and happiness and a smile to their faces.

Negative Energy Traits: This Leo has a highly sensitive ego and often seeks the approval of others. They hate to be perceived as weak and therefore have a hard time saying no. They want to be there for everyone all the time. This Leo also loves to dominate conversations, and, because they are so busy talking, they often forget to listen. Sometimes this is seen as attention-seeking.

Leo of Second Decan: August 2–12
Ruled by Jupiter.

Positive Energy Traits: Risk takers and motivated. This Leo loves the spotlight and flourishes when they can be the leader instead of the follower. They love to offer their old-soul-like advice with positive support and a dose of reality. They have a wisdom that spans beyond their earthly years. This Leo loves to dig into the unknown—whether learning a foreign language, cooking up an international recipe, or traveling to an exotic location. This Leo daydreams of moving across the country, or out of the country, but is torn because they also love to be around their family.

Negative Energy Traits: Easily frustrated, mouthy, moody, and lacks self-esteem. This cat can roar without thinking first. They rarely will apologize or admit they are wrong. This Leo is ambitious but has a hard time doing what they do for future finances. They love to spend money, often buying trinkets for their friends and family instead of saving for the future.

Leo of Third Decan: August 13–23
Ruled by Mars.

Positive Energy Traits: This Leo loves to jump into a new project with confidence and an inextinguishable drive to excel. Never accepting defeat, their feisty and daring energy will continue to fight until the challenge is successfully achieved. This Leo likes to rule the jungle, being the ultimate boss. Loyalty is what this Leo defines as romance. They are chivalrous and hopeless romantics.

Negative Energy Traits: Temperamental, stubborn, and frugal, this Leo gets into a slow-as-a-sloth-type mood and nobody can motivate them out of their space. They get bored and hate anything repetitive, spouting their moodiness at everyone else, all the while not doing anything to change it.

July Leo vs. August Leo

Along with each sign being split into their third decans, there is a difference between each zodiac split between the months.

July Leo gets frustrated easily.

August Leo will get frustrated but tries not to show it.

July Leo is brave and headstrong.

August Leo will battle for what they want.

July Leo is proud.

August Leo is stubborn proud.

July Leo is sweet and flirty.

August Leo is fierce and flirty.

July Leo has a hard time balancing their finances.

August Leo over-budgets and overthinks the finances.

Leo Masculine and Feminine Energy

Energy has a yin and yang that is interpreted as feminine and masculine, and according to the energy it is explained below:

Feminine July Leo: The feminine energy of a Leo in July is proud, independent, and motivated—the typical Leo stereotype. They don't want to be atypical, instead trying to find their uniqueness and specialness. They can become anxious and frustrated when trying to figure out their lives. Put their best friend in front of them, though, and they can share intuitive and strong advice, all while wishing they could move forward in the same.

Masculine July Leo: The masculine energy of Leo in July is self-driven and motivated. They can be demeaning and self-righteous, sharing their opinions as gospel. They love to be the boss and demand that their way is the right way. Although they come across as self-assured, they are really filled with doubt and just don't want anyone to see their true selves.

Feminine August Leo: The feminine energy of a Leo in August is headstrong. They don't want anyone to know their secrets but will flaunt their rage with a moody temper. But be careful if this Leo goes into silent mode; it could be they are planning for world domination or falling apart and don't want anyone to see. Don't bother asking because their response will always be "I'm fine"; they don't want to be a burden to anyone. An hour later they'll likely divulge, but it's on their terms and in their own time.

Masculine August Leo: The masculine energy of a Leo in August struts as a boss. They are arrogant and cocky without apology. For many it's an act because they like emotional privacy. They are loving and fun to talk to when in the mood to talk.

They are loyal, sometimes to a fault as they don't love to make changes, especially with regard to career.

Leo Positive Traits

Passionate

The Leo has natural showmanship, sharing warmth and heart with everyone they meet. The Leo rules not only their kingdom but everyone else's, wanted or not; but it's done with good intention. With a speech ready on a whim's notice, they are ready to motivate. The Leo can inspire even when you didn't realize you needed inspiration. They have a way of drawing you into their world, all the while taking care of their subjects (which is everyone). Leo does everything with flair, costumes optional. Well, sometimes optional.

Creative

Get the karaoke machine ready, the Leo is always ready to bedazzle the world with their sassy attitude while adorned with shiny sequins. The Leo loves to channel their inner star and be adored and adorned, whether it's for their grocery shopping abilities or work skills. Leo's creative expressions in any field touch emotions and bring them into the limelight as a leader or a role model. Everything they do is creative, offering a unique contribution to the world.

Trustworthy

The Leo understands that steadiness is the key and reliability and loyalty aid in their true happiness. Leos are stable, determined, and resolute. They want to get to the finish line and want others to succeed with them. If a Leo makes a promise, they will do all in their power to keep that promise, and they prefer a handshake over a piece of paper.

Leo Negative Traits

Moody

A Leo sulks like nobody else. Everything they do is intense and dramatic, including their feelings. We all know that the Leo likes to be the center of attention, even if it's by throwing a temper tantrum. Whether it's road rage or an argument of passion, it's hard to ignore their moodiness. The Leo is a fire sign and has an enthusiastic energy; because of this they burn out rapidly and need time to decompress or else you will hear the roar.

Complicated

Although Leos may appear to be tremendously self-assured, bubbling with confidence, and with a long line of fans wanting to spend time in their presence, they are complicated. They are stubborn, and it's hard to change their ways since they believe their way is the best way. They have an ego that needs to be stroked, and like a typical cat you can pet here and there but if you make a mistake and pet there then you will hear about it. And then the next day they want to know why you are upset with them. They will dance around a situation in indecision, all the while pretending to be confident.

Lazy

The Leo likes to lie around and snore after all their roaring and strutting. Don't try to motivate a Leo when they get into this space or you'll likely face a very angry kitty cat—and don't count on any purring. The Leo is the king or queen of the zodiac and goes into a *peel me grapes and feed them to me* mood. Their need for adoration without doing anything to win it over can look arrogant and self-righteous.

Leo Keywords

proud

BOSSY

CONFIDENT

stubborn

generous

ROYAL

DEMANDING   strong

Leo Communication Style

A Leo believes they are the best communicator and should be awarded and admired for such. Leos, though, must be in the mood to communicate and the subject must interest them, keep their attention, and continue being relevant. It is the Leo that wants to command the topic, the mood, and the tone. The Leo can chameleon from serious to dramatic on a moment's notice. When speaking with a Leo, be sure to validate if not applaud them throughout the conversation.

Leo Misconceptions

The Leo energy is often known for being the center of attention and loving to spend money. But not all embrace those traits, and they can be frugal with how they spend.

Leos strut around looking strong and confident, as if they don't need anyone or anything. The big secret of the Leo is that they simply want to be needed and loved. Drawing the attention to themselves can look arrogant, but it's not meant to be narcissistic; it's simply the only way they know to gesture for love and adoration. Leo can be one of the most loving and thoughtful people.

Don't Be a Leo, Leo

The world is your stage, Leo, and everyone is part of your entourage. Or at least that's what you'd like to believe. Everyone knows you like to be the center of attention, even as you play shy and coy and pretend that you don't want to be the center of attention. It's part of the drama you write. Your lesson, Leo, is that no matter what part you are given in life, it truly is an important part. Let others have the lead sometimes. I know it's hard, but you will find that you are the showstopper no matter what.

Thoughts from a Leo

A Cusper

Cuspers take on the energy of the zodiac signs they hover between—the good and the bad of both—making them both complicated and intriguing.

"It never surprised me that Cancer's animal is the crab. Between mood swings and sensitivity, I am known to get a bit 'crabby' at times—probably more than I care to admit. However, while some may consider these traits to be weaknesses, I choose to embrace them. My sensitivity has taught me compassion and empathy. My ever-changing moods have taught me adaptability. Being on the cusp of Leo (July 21), I have a constant battle between water and fire, but this isn't necessarily a bad thing. I have some Leo traits that help to balance things out a bit. My Cancer side wants to cry and nurture those in need, but my Leo side wants to find whoever is responsible for hurting them and bring them to justice. I am reserved, yet feisty. While my Cancer traits are dominant, I think the Leo in me helps to keep me from being taken advantage of, and also helps with my sense of style: I like to dress to impress. While the Cancer in me wants to hide away, the Leo in me wants to steal just a bit of the spotlight."

—Christi

The Comedian

When thinking of a Leo energy, being funny isn't one of the traits that immediately comes to mind, but it is a trait that many have. Sometimes it's about being the center of attention, but other times it's a safe way to help send healing to another.

"When I was younger, I was always the life of the party. Now that I am older, I have become much more reserved … and I'm not necessarily happy about it. My favorite sound is a friend's laughter. As a comedian, the laughter I heard coming from the audience was the most beautiful sound on Earth. I called it 'music of the soul.'

I often joke that I can't handle more than five minutes of seriousness at a time. It may be more like three-and-a-half minutes. This can be frustrating for the serious people in my world, but as my type of Leo, that's their problem. I don't care if you are laughing at me or with me, as long as you are laughing."

—Mikey

An Overload of Emotions

A Leo has a gambit of emotions that doesn't just exhaust those who love them, but it exhausts themselves too.

"There are good and bad points to being a Leo. We're overwhelmed easily and we need time to panic, but once we have that time we get stuff done. We need to be recognized. It doesn't have to be anything big, but the recognition is important. We're judgmental until we know you, but once we do, we're incredibly accepting—to the point where we get screwed over. But one too many times and you've lost an incredible friend. We like to please others, but we want that thoughtfulness returned. We're incredibly melodramatic and overly emotional, but we love with everything we have. We like attention. We don't need to be the center of everyone's attention, but we want to be listened to. We're creative and love to give elaborate, well-thought-out gifts. We're fiercely loyal to the point that we get defensive and stubborn. We love hard and want to make the people that we love happy."

—Micaela

Leo and Relationships

Strengths

Leos do have a special honesty that draws people into their world. They are charismatic, cuddly, and passionate. Always ready to create and explore, the Leo loves to be the hero in the relationship, whether baking cookies for a significant other's office or balancing the budget for parents. They truly want to help, hoping to get a pat on the back, all the while pretending they don't need or want it. The Leo is sexual and flirtatious, curious and engaging.

Challenges

The Leo is afraid of being vulnerable and can hide their true selves behind white lies. The scenes they write themselves in can become so convincing that they believe their own fibs. They are also extremely demanding of themselves and of those they allow to walk in their jungle, leading to unrealistic expectations, jealousies, and an overbearing attitude.

Leo in the Workplace

Strengths

The Leo boss is a hard worker that delegates well. They stick up for those who show loyalty and are good team players. Leos make natural leaders who are driven and determined. The Leo boss likes to have fun and is encouraging, offering praise and reassurances. They will listen to your ideas with attention and constructive criticism. The Leo boss wants their employees to excel by being a mentor, a teacher, and a friend. They are natural salespeople, with amazing persuasion qualities.

Challenges

The Leo boss loves to waste time by looking as busy as can be. They demand to be respected, rarely compromise, and will gossip with the employees in order to find out information that can later be used against them.

Parenting a Leo Child

Make sure to pour on the purrs for your Leo child. They need encouragement and guidance to stay their course, and of course they need honest praise and applause.

Strengths

Leader of the Pack: They aren't a fan favorite of bullies and will protect their pack. The Leo child will take the lead, and typically won't fall victim to peer pressure. The Leo will have a variety of friends from different groups that will come from their wide range of interests, from drama to debate. They are passionate and crave to be seen in an individualistic way. The Leo is born to be a leader and with that comes traits such as kindness, fairness, and honesty.

Love Responsibility: The Leo child loves responsibility as long as it interests them; they don't want to be bored, but they do need their down, lazy time.

Warm and Loving: Leos want to be admired and adored, and in exchange will shine their love on those who love them unconditionally.

Artistic: The Leo child loves to explore their creative side. Don't be surprised to wake up one morning and find they've decorated their walls with crayons and markers, and they'll be very proud of their inner Picasso.

Challenges

Varying Moods: Leo energies express all their emotions from happiness to dislikes, excitement to dissatisfactions. They can be easily frustrated and impatient one minute and giggling and content the next.

Temper: The Leo child is prone to temper tantrums, normally as a way of voicing their frustrations and the varying moods that rock like a pendulum. If things don't go the way they envision it to go, they may growl or simply go for the full-out roar.

Anxious to Get Older: A Leo child is anxious to not be treated like a child. They tend to hang in groups of people older than them.

Leo as a Parent

Strengths

Fiercely Protective: The Leo parent will protect their cub before asking questions. It's a sign of true loyalty and love.

Encouragers: The Leo parent is an amazing encourager, helping to motivate, mentor, and teach their child how to express their own individuality.

Softies: The Leo parent may try to impress with their tougher-than-nails exterior, but they are quite loving and warm. Their roar is louder than their actual bite.

Generous: The Leo parent may show attitude, act judgmental, and look disagreeable when asking for something, but the Leo is very generous and will give in without too much pressure.

Challenges

The Boss: The Leo parent is the boss no matter what, and don't try to convince the lion otherwise, because you won't win.

Self-Centered: The Leo is the center of the universe, whether a child, parent, or boss. It's about what they want first and foremost.

Private: The Leo parent is chatty and social, but they don't want to dump all their problems out for the public to pick through. You'll likely hear the stories they want to share, but not all the stories.

Temperamental: Sure, they are moody. They get frustrated. They work themselves hard and others pay for it with their temper.

Leo and Finances

Leos have a taste for luxury, loving high-end and upscale items. During their younger years they may find themselves impulsive with spending. As they age, they find their way of budgeting, comparing prices, and becoming sensible. They are always generous and also entrepreneurial. They will figure out how to generate more income to continue to be stable and generous.

Moon in Leo

The Leo moon acts as an extra oomph of self-confidence and helps you take the leap to go after what calls to you—taking chances, having faith, and believing! If you've felt stalled, this energy will give you the push you need.

New Moon in Leo

Each one of us carries scars from the past, but it's all how we display them that hurts or helps us. This New Moon reminds you that it's okay to be scared and overwhelmed, but be careful to not overthink. You might be trying to please everyone, forgetting that you need to be happy too. This moon reminds you to try to just have faith and not wonder how, what, or why things can get better. Just believe that the mess all around you and the thoughts circling in your head will be sorted out; it just doesn't have to be now. And it doesn't have to be tomorrow either. However, carrying the wounds from the past can damage your ability to actually move forward. This moon is powerful and can help you push through and find peace, forgiveness, and rediscovering your ROAR. Choosing your thoughts sets a course for your future.

This is a time to have self-confidence and go after what calls to you—taking chances, having faith, and believing! If you've felt stalled, this moon will give you the push you need. So get out your garden tools and begin weeding your own emotional jungle.

This Energy in Leo is Great for:
Setting goals.

Exploring new romance (or relighting the flame of a current romance).

Organizing your home, office, and/or car.

Fighting for what you want in your life.

Embracing and releasing your inner child.

Full Moon in Leo
Your life is much like a secret garden—you have to make time to look for the keys, the doorways, and the beauty within you. So often we look outside of ourselves to feel happiness, when really it is within us. Our birthright vibration gets misplaced and we blame outsiders, sometimes victimizing. The Leo Full Moon is a time to discover you again. You might have some weeding to do, you might have some resting to do, but the hard work will pay off in the end. It's up to you to find the in-between of snoring and roaring.

The Full Moon in Leo reminds us of our inner playful and childlike energy. The moon ignites the spiritual flame and releases the blockages to find our curiousity, our joy, and our love.

Full Moons are like mirrors for your soul. Everything is exposed and that can sometimes be tough, especially in a Leo energy. This moon is about pushing fear out of the way, though, and learning to be kind to yourself. Practice your purr and your roar and take your place back in your jungle.

Soul Work
Strive to listen with patience and give those around you a chance to speak. Also, keep in mind that while being candid in your delivery is a mighty good quality, it is necessary to censor or phrase your words to avoid being misinterpreted by the narrow-minded and conservative thinkers in your midst.

Now Is the Time
Do set goals for ways to move forward. Don't beat yourself up over goals undone. Prioritize movement in life (possibly even real estate moving too). Don't lay around waiting for the rest of your pride to do all the work. Do organize your home, office, and car. Don't shuffle your stuff around to make it look temporarily neat and orderly. Do add some creative work to your life. Don't get frustrated by looking at all the work you have to do in your life; take it project by project.

Leo Totem Animal

Unicorn
The Leo energy embraces the unicorn totem. The unicorn embraces the magic of what might not be seen, and dreams of what

might be. The unicorn stands out in the crowd, sparkling and unique. The unicorn is also giving, creative, loyal, and loving.

The unicorn offers a gift of:

Creativity

Magic

Beauty

Mystery

Dreaming

six

VIRGO

August 23–September 22
Earth Energy ♍

Virgos are conservative, organized, and practical; their symbol is the maiden. They do well when life is methodical and planned, with nothing being left to chance. They despise chaos and would rather everything in their lives and the lives of others stay within the lines, with the borders truly defined.

The Virgo energy is constantly worried. They worry they will miss details or someone else around them won't meet the standards they've set. They expect the worst and wonder why their world sucks when they manifest the same. It's easy for the Virgo to get into a negative mindset with a lot of brain overflow. The Virgo can often come across as critical, sarcastic, and insensitive. The Virgo isn't mean, though; they just want it their way and feel their way is the only way. Sure, it comes across as controlling, but a Virgo lives their best life when everything falls into place the way they see it should.

Virgo energies succeed when the smallest details are checked off and flow nicely in a successful way.

Virgos are deeply rooted in helping. They are feelers and have a tender heart. They love to experience moments, just in a very planned way. It could be toes in the water to breathing in the sea air. Or sitting in a whitewashed chair with a cold lemonade in the countryside. Or simply wearing the most comfortable jeans, white cotton oversized t-shirt, no makeup, and reading a good book. The Virgo energy loves to make contributions to experiences and share that with the ones they love.

Virgo Decans

Each zodiac is broken down into triplicities, each having their own energy added to their zodiac sign. This is Virgo broken down:

Virgo of First Decan: August 23–September 3
Ruled by Mercury.

Positive Energy Traits: This Virgo is romantic, sensitive, and thoughtful. They wear their heart on their sleeve and are sometimes embarrassed by it. They want loyalty and love. They are the ones who check in with their mom. Whether male or female energy, they will bring their family or best friends hot chicken soup and a teddy bear to cheer them up when ill. It's that type of sensitivity that makes them lovable. This Virgo does love adventure and travel.

Negative Energy Traits: This Virgo is emotionally a mess. They are moody and depressed. You will often find them brooding about this, that, and more of this. They like life to go their way. Anything that happens out of the way they see it should be will be met by brooding.

Virgo of Second Decan: September 4–13
Ruled by Saturn.

Positive Energy Traits: This Virgo loves security and safety. They are amazing organizers and managers. They are respectful and tactful. This Virgo isn't a fan of frivolously spending money and can figure out how to make money and then budget appropriately. They are gentle, sympathetic, and wonderful listeners.

Negative Energy Traits: This Virgo doesn't like to ask for help and is every bit of a perfectionist to the core. Others look at them as mentors, which is often a heavy weight. They don't want to admit they are wrong when they are, and an apology is hard to get out of them. They are overly critical of others, and even more critical of themselves.

Virgo of Third Decan: September 14–22
Ruled by Venus.

Positive Energy Traits: This Virgo is considerably creative. They make amazing musicians, writers, cinematic producers, and so on. They have an artistic flair and apply this to everything from their home to their personal style and their words. This Virgo is a romantic and they fall in love quickly, truly believing in a forever love and soulmates. This energy is also very psychic and will feel out the room as to whom to trust and not, and often trusts their *spidey senses* even if there isn't a black-and-white reasoning with it.

Negative Energy Traits: This Virgo is quiet and reserved. They don't love to take risks, are rarely spontaneous, and prefer routine. You will find an unhappy Virgo when you put a restriction on their life. Even though they like things just the way they like them doesn't mean they will be happy if someone else tries to put up a boundary.

August Virgo vs. September Virgo

Along with each sign being split into their third decans, there is a difference between each zodiac split between the months.

The August Virgo is loud.

The September Virgo is quiet.

The August Virgo is aggressive.

The September Virgo is passive-aggressive.

The August Virgo is social and outgoing but
often fakes it well.

The September Virgo likes to be a homebody
and would rather not fake it.

The August Virgo loves drama and attention.

The September Virgo would rather blend in.

The August Virgo is pretty patient and laid back.

The September Virgo is impatient and tense.

The August Virgo can be an obstinate know-it-all.

The September Virgo is bossy.

The August Virgo has a quirky sense of humor.

The September Virgo can come across as dismissive.

Virgo Masculine and Feminine Energy

Energy has a yin and yang that is interpreted as feminine and masculine, and according to the energy it is explained below:

Feminine August Virgo: The feminine energy of a Virgo in August is determined and capable of holding up the world. Only a select few will know everything that's going on in this Virgo's life. They are so busy taking care of everyone and everything; they have constant to-do lists in their heads and often feel overwhelmed. And their loved ones wonder why they are moody and flustered. They want everything to be perfect; and we all know there will never be perfection.

Masculine August Virgo: The masculine energy of a Virgo in August loves to pretend to keep it real. They want to be seen as chill and easygoing, all the while being a worry-wart—always questioning and digging. They try to hide an inner Jekyll/Hyde. They are articulate with communication and love to be social and experience adventures.

Feminine September Virgo: The feminine energy of a Virgo in September is hyper-awake, noticing everything going on around them. They like to make the best out of the best and seeing through the worst to make the best. They know how to balance the good times with the work times. They are driven, smart, cautious, and sensitive.

Masculine September Virgo: The masculine energy of a Virgo in September is a hard worker. They are always looking at ways to improve their lives and the lives of their loved ones. They seek perfect harmony and are devoted to friends and family. They do get stressed when others aren't pulling their weight and don't know how to communicate it except for pouting and moodiness.

Virgo Positive Traits

Reliable
Virgos are reliable and timely. They are often the first to be at work, and the last to be punching out, and somehow fit in grocery shopping, attending a memorial service, and budgeting the next

ten years for themselves and their whole family. They try to make overachievement look natural.

Practical

Virgos are not riding through life on a unicorn, in a make-believe world. They are realistic and pragmatic. If you want the truth with no frills, you ask a Virgo. They have a great sense of humor; it's just different, and sometimes surprising.

Kind

Virgos are caring and giving, although they may not show their true expressions. They want to be perceived as logical, and they are. They are afraid, though, that if they show kindness, it takes away their practicality; so they dismiss it when called out on it. But Virgo is kind and loving.

Virgo Negative Traits

Opinionated

Virgos have many opinions about a variety of situations. They analyze, research, and talk to others about topics, sometimes becoming bogged down with too much information and not seeing the larger picture. Virgos can pick and choose the details they want to focus on, becoming opinionated on what they've chosen to see as their reality. Their opinions can be expressed in a cynical, sarcastic, and hurtful way.

Critical

The Virgo visualizes how they see the following should go: their day, their year, their romance, their job, their children, parenting, and every other part of their life. Nothing in life goes exactly as planned, but in a Virgo's world that is exactly what they want to happen. When their plotting and planning goes astray and the plan isn't executed precisely, you will see a very stressed Virgo. Instead of taking responsibility, or going with the flow, the critical part of the Virgo will turn into the Incredible Hulk, spewing a short temper and criticism.

Worriers

Virgo energy can turn on a dime, mostly due to anxiety. Depending upon their mood and the environment, they are sometimes seen as wishy-washy. They make plans for a Friday on a Wednesday and cancel plans for Friday on a Thursday, just a day after making them. It can be exhausting for those who love a Virgo, because even though the Virgo wants routine, they may not offer others the same consistency in the name of worrying and anxiety.

Virgo Keywords

overwhelmed   HELPERS

self-destructive

healers

ORGANIZED

RESOURCEFUL

Virgo Communication Style

Virgos need you to stick to the facts and be as exact and as detailed as possible without any frills or fancy. If possible, if you can skip the beginning, the middle, and just get to the ending, it would be even better for them. They love to add their two cents in the name of helpfulness. Their advice can come across as judgmental and critical, though. Virgos will often make silent demands, thinking you are psychic or can pick up on their cues. When you don't, you will see one sad Virgo.

Virgo Misconceptions

Virgos often struggle with their own attributes and misconceptions. They are often seen as dull and stuffy, cheap, and disenchanted. Although they do like to be practical, they are witty and often sarcastic. They like to look at life issues and find humor in them.

Don't Be a Virgo, Virgo

It isn't just exhausting for you, Virgo, to be the perfectionist, detail-oriented, always the over-achiever; it's exhausting for everyone else too. You know that person who is always raising their hand in school or at the work meeting, either proving their smarts, adding nonsense to the content, or panicked because they need more details? That's you, Virgo. That's YOU. It sometimes looks neurotic and it's maddening. Your lesson, Virgo, is to start trusting yourself. Know that mistakes are okay, and stop worrying about what others think. Take some deep breaths and be.

Thoughts from a Virgo

A Struggle of Balance

Each sign has a dash of the astrological attributes of the sign before and after it.

> "I am lightning when it startles the sky and shakes the earth. A constant struggle for balance between the deep need for alone time and a desire to shine brightly as the center of attention. I prefer being large and in charge, but tire of the responsibility and crave the mundane. I am the loyal Leo and a leader—courageous and energetic, fierce and charming. I am a private, quiet Virgo with intimacy issues. Virgo allows me to be calm, too cool sometimes, and quite collected. I bounce between introvert and extrovert. I've learned over the years to embrace my inner Leo and put those skills to good use, creating a business and marketing plan for myself. I always felt more Virgo—the creative author and artist—but my passion, drive, and tenacity are all Leo. I even wear yellow and orange now to honor all of me."
>
> —Richey

Stability and Perfection

Virgos are loyal if you are loyal to them and are happiest when everything is exactly the way they want it to be.

> "Many have said that Virgo is an aloof, control-freak perfectionist. Virgos are so much more than that. Sure, we like our things organized, and yours too! We can be crabby if our environment isn't just so. Deal with

it, 'cause once we are comfortable with you, we are loyal, would do anything for you, and are witty as hell. We just want everything in order and everyone to get along! I've been married to the same man for thirty years. Every job I have ever held, I've been told that I'm great at organizing and I bring a sense of stability. I work hard at being the best teacher I can be. If there is something to worry about, I'll find it. Yeah, all Virgo traits. But look past the control freak and take the aloofness for what it is—shyness."

—Dayna

Nurturers

Virgos love to help, but it typically has to be their way of helping because their way of helping is the right way, according to a Virgo.

"Although Virgos are considered control freaks, we are really nurturers with control-freak attributes. Virgos are famous for having an eye for detail. They know how to read between the lines and problem-solve a spreadsheet or mediate coworkers' disagreements. You don't have to do everything we say to do, but it would be advised to do everything we say to do."

—Kim

Virgo and Relationships

Strengths

Dedicated: Virgos hold everyone they love close to them. Whether a romantic interest, a friend, or a family member, they are more than willing to be by your side, morning, noon, or night, holding your hand and helping wherever they can. The Virgo will love you at your worst and your best and won't run away unless you push them away.

Consistent: Because of the Virgo's practicality, they are dependable and routine with their words and their actions. If you make them feel important, they will be your forever cheerleader. Just know that a Virgo doesn't always demonstrate their love from an emotional place. Instead, their love language might be taking your car to fill it with gasoline and an oil change. They don't play games with love and expect those they love to respect that in return.

Romantic: Many Virgos appear shy and reserved in the beginning, but Virgos are romantic and sexy. A Virgo isn't complicated in any part of their life, romance included. Offer a Virgo security and some freedom, give them compliments and communicate—then the Virgo will stick by your side forever. A Virgo will always be a dedicated spouse, and though predictable, they have a wild and romantic side that could surprise you. They do like to be affectionate and like their partner to be as well.

Challenges

Financially Impulsive: It may be surprising to find out that the Virgo, so methodical and routine, is often financially impulsive. Although they set themselves up for financial stability, they enjoy spending money on luxury items. The challenge is that they are embarrassed or afraid of criticism, so they hide it from their partner until it can't be an avoided topic.

Critical: The Virgo doesn't even realize that they can be so critical. It's not so much toward others, but more toward themselves, being their own worst enemy. A true definition of cup half empty, the Virgo can be told all day everyday how wonderful and smart they are, but they will find their flaws. Stay out of their way when they get into their moods. In that moment they will be skeptical of anything and everything.

Needy: A Virgo is needy. They need alone time. They need you to tell them you love them on a regular basis. They need you to not lie to them. They need you to not play mind games. They need you to not drift away from them. They need time with their friends. They need routine and for you to understand that what they need to do is to be methodical, and to understand that their way, according to them, is the right way.

Virgo in the Workplace

Strengths

A Virgo boss is literal and concise, analytical and hard-working. They like facts and figures. They despise excuses unless backed with logic, and even then can be unsympathetic and cold. So sure, you might have to call in sick because of the flu, but if you aren't dying from the flu don't expect any pity. They value time and they won't be hanging around the water cooler talking about the television show drama from the night before. They also won't love their employees hanging around the water cooler either.

Challenges

A Virgo boss is a micromanager who will criticize every suggestion and every move made. They have been known to dismiss an idea and then come up with the same idea and call it amazing. The Virgo boss is a perfectionist and nitpicker. As long as you stay helpful and double-check your own work, there will rarely be a problem.

Parenting a Virgo Child

Virgos are naturally critical of themselves. They rarely need to be micromanaged as they are so busy managing themselves, and others too. They have common sense and are detail-oriented, carefully weighing their pros and cons. They want to learn and want you to teach them. So be patient and spend time helping them help you. It might be quicker for you to cook the dinner but let them help. And it might take you an hour to cut the grass while it takes them three hours, but they will try to do the best job. Let them.

Strengths

Hardworking: The Virgo child is motivated by anything that will make them feel like an adult. Give the Virgo chores such as laundry, cooking, or cleaning and watch them excel. Offer them an allowance for said chores and they will soar. The Virgo child/teenager will attempt to find a job early in childhood, dishing out ice cream at the local ice cream parlor, babysitting, or mowing lawns to earn money.

Smart: Your Virgo child is intelligent. They have an uncanny way of seeing what others don't, paying attention to small details. They pick up on academics quickly and love to be stimulated in advanced classes.

Independent: The Virgo child is laid back and happy. They have an older soul, wanting to please and blend into the background, not wanting to be a problem. They love their independence and will try to earn their parents' trust with responsibility.

Challenges

Sensitive: Virgo is a sensitive child who is hardly any problem, and fades into the background of the family dynamic. It's important to allow the Virgo child downtime, but don't assume that since they aren't causing any issues they don't need your time and energy. They also retreat if they feel teased or feel inferior. They can dish it but can rarely take it.

Space: Make sure to give your Virgo child some space. They don't like being backed into a corner by being bombarded with questions. Because they are so sensitive, they need their space so they can deal with their emotions and decompress the day away. There is often a lot going on in their head and they will paint the picture that everything is going great in their life. It's a fine line with a Virgo, respecting their sensitivity and their space. If you offer them a happy medium of space, they will happily confide in you.

Picky: The Virgo child is picky with what foods they eat. They are picky about what clothes they put on. They are picky about their group of friends. They are plain picky. It can be exhausting to please them as they will express their displeasure but won't explain what they do want.

Virgo as a Parent

Strengths

Laid Back: Don't be surprised if the child of a Virgo says they get dessert before dinner, as long as all their veggies are eaten. The Virgo parent is routine, but they pick and choose what they decide is worth fighting.

Adventurous: Virgo parents like to travel and find adventure in even little outings to the mall or the park. The Virgo parent will set up a camping trip to the living room or backyard.

Encouraging: The Virgo parent truly wants the best of the best for their child. They will encourage, support, and love their child into their fullest potential. Sometimes seen as criticism, it is done in the name of encouragement, according to a Virgo.

Challenges

Demanding: The Virgo parent pushes their child; although it's done in the name of love, it can sometimes come across as critical. The Virgo parent wants everything perfect, the way they see it should be, and there isn't a lot of wiggle room in their mind. Not only is that not realistic, it's exhausting.

Uncommunicative: The Virgo parent isn't always clear about what they need and want, adding confusion and disorder, and creating arguments as the child gets older.

Suffocating: The Virgo parent wants to know everything that is going on in their child's life, suspicious especially when everything is going just fine. They will be the one sneaking around in their children's room and electronics, looking for something to use against them. It's not that they don't trust their child; they just want to make sure their child is safe.

Virgo and Finances

Virgos are practical. They pinch pennies and have been called cheap, or more kindly called frugal. They are hardworking, but also like to figure out how to make money by hardly working. They do like their money, so don't try to borrow it from them, or else they will hold that above you forever. The Virgo will splurge, though, but it often comes with buyer's remorse.

Moon in Virgo

The Virgo energy helps us discover the personal power we've always had but forgot was there or forgot how to use. It's a healing energy that mends the wounds on the soul, reminding you that cobwebs look great for Halloween but not in your life. The Virgo energy hands you the duster and tells you to get to work.

New Moon in Virgo

It's a time to look at ways you can put yourself first. Do you even remember? If not, maybe take a second and write down all the things you love or might have loved. Opening the doorway even just a little lets some light in.

What to Watch for during the Virgo New Moon:

Frustration when perfection isn't achieved.

A higher sense of energy.

Increased security and loyalty.

Lack of communication.

Since this moon is in Virgo, you may feel frustrated and stressed, and you may second-guess yourself. It would do you good to push that aside. This is a good time to clean the house, declutter the closets, and most of all, wash the cobwebs from your wishes and dreams.

Full Moon in Virgo

Virgo projects a powerful energy of self-doubt in all aspects of life, which can make the most confident person want to pull the blankets over their head. The best way to deal with this moon is to hide. Okay, not really, but you may feel like that is for the best.

If you can't do that, do your best to avoid conflict and negativity, and to be aware of communication and interactions with others, ignoring that voice inside your head.

For several days you may feel as if you aren't in control of your life—as if someone stole your life's GPS. Blasts from the past may challenge you, in both a physical and an emotional way. So, if you're out at a bar and you see your ex with a sexy someone, don't make a scene, even in your head! These encounters might be hurtful and emotional, but Full Moons are all about release. We so often bury the past instead of letting it go. It's time to let it go. Full Moons are about releasing, and this is a powerful one to remind us to do just that.

Although this Full Moon may spotlight more negativity than positivity, on the surface, just know that sometimes the story in your head creates several flying monkeys and wicked witches when there are really none. So, change your story, and make sure to not make yourself a victim.

By taking some extra time to understand what others are saying to you, and what you are saying to you, you will survive this Full Moon.

Soul Work

Listen to your inner voice. Meditation is a great way to turn up your inner voice and intuition to tune in. This meditation can help you during the new or the Full Moon.

Find a place that is quiet and comfortable. Let your eyes close and begin to take deep breaths in and out, focusing on your breathing, all the while letting your thoughts drift out of your mind.

Focus your awareness on the body. As you continue your deep breathing, deepen your sense of relaxation. Notice if there is a heavier feeling in any part of your body. Is your throat tightening? Or maybe your stomach feels heavy? Are you getting pins and needles in your feet?

Visualize a bright white light coming down from the ceiling and wrapping that healing light around you. Send some extra light to the heavier parts of your body too.

Continue to rest. It is during this rest that you can begin to tune in to your inner voice.

Ask out loud or in your mind, "What do I need to be aware of or know right now?" Be open to the response.

You might have thoughts, images, or feelings. Be receptive to them and accept what you receive. If you don't hear, see, or feel a response, it may be delayed and come later in your waking or dream state.

When you are ready, notice your breath, wiggle your toes and fingers, gradually have a stretch, and come back to the room.

Some feel asking a question that requires a simple "yes" or "no" in meditation is easier.

Find a place that is quiet and comfortable. Let your eyes close and begin to take deep breaths in and out, focusing on your breathing, all the while letting your thoughts drift out of your mind.

Focus your awareness on the body. As you continue your deep breathing, deepen your sense of relaxation. Notice if there is a heavier feeling in any part of your body. Is your throat tightening? Or maybe your stomach is feeling heavy? Are you getting pins and needles in your feet?

Visualize a bright white light coming down from the ceiling and wrapping that healing light around you. Remember to send some extra light to the heavier parts of your body.

Continue to rest. It is during this rest that you can begin to tune in to your inner voice.

Ask your "yes" or "no" question.

Be open to the response. You might have thoughts, images, or feelings. Be receptive to them and accept what you receive. You can also program yourself to know your "yes" or "no." You might see a flower, feel a sense of joy or relief, or hear happy music with your "yes." With your "no" you might see an elephant (elephant in the room) or a storm, feel a sense of dread, or hear somber music.

If you don't hear, see, or feel a response, it may be delayed and come later in your waking or dream state.

When you are ready, notice your breath, wiggle your toes and fingers, gradually have a stretch, and come back to the room.

Things to Do during This Full Moon:

Do watch a comedy. Don't start an argument. Do go to yoga. Don't take others' negativity personally. Do focus on solutions. Don't focus on problems. Do journal. Don't surround yourself with negative people. Do make a vision board. Don't talk about serious things (money, politics, engagement rings, etc.).

Virgo Totem Animal

Bear

The Virgo energy embraces the bear totem. The bear embraces the deepest part of your energy. Although they look snuggly and many want to hug a bear, a bear may not want to be hugged—needing space and independence. A bear can be modest, reclusive, lazy, and grumbly. Give them time to hibernate and recenter themselves. Once the bear crawls from their place, watch the bear be generous, hardworking, and observant.

The bear offers a gift of:

Independence

Perfectionism

Grumpiness

Methodical

Intelligence

Big-hearted

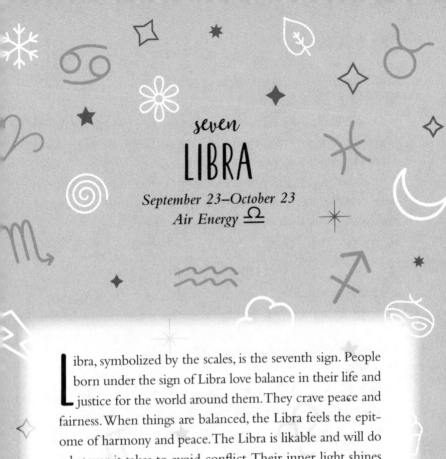

seven
LIBRA

September 23–October 23
Air Energy ♎

L ibra, symbolized by the scales, is the seventh sign. People born under the sign of Libra love balance in their life and justice for the world around them. They crave peace and fairness. When things are balanced, the Libra feels the epitome of harmony and peace. The Libra is likable and will do whatever it takes to avoid conflict. Their inner light shines brightly, and people are enamored by their energy. They can gather a group of people around them, make friends easily, and draw attention with humbled admiration. They are intelligent but will hide it so as not to come across as intimidating. They want to blend in.

This sign is easygoing, creative, and artistic. They don't care what group they belong to and would much rather belong to all the groups, without prejudice. The Libra loves everything beautiful and will fuss over their home environment and their own personal style, pretending all the

117

while that it didn't take them long at all to find the perfect dress or decorate for the holidays.

You'll likely see a Libra try to find their Zen by writing, dancing, yoga, or some type of physical exercise. You'll also likely see a Libra hugging a dog or cuddling a cat. This energy loves to root for the underdog and sometimes it is truly the furry kind. Charitable causes are near and dear to their heart, but they are humble and won't flaunt their big heart or giving wallet.

Libra Decans

Each zodiac is broken down into triplicities, each having their own energy added to their zodiac sign. This is Libra broken down:

Libra of First Decan: September 23–October 3
Ruled by Venus.

Positive Energy Traits: This Libra loves to embrace their inner hippie, but just because they love all things love, harmony, and peace doesn't mean they are naïve or stupid. This Libra is intelligent, imaginative, and intuitive. They love beauty and everything creative, and are wonderful in an occupation in film, culinary arts, writing, or graphic design. If a new restaurant is opening—they're there. On opening night of the newest blockbuster movie—they're there. Anything that might heighten their senses is in their perfect vibe. Another thing this Libra loves is romance. They love to be loved and love to love in return. This Libra is friendly, sociable, and fun-loving, and loves romance with fancy and folly.

Negative Energy Traits: This Libra is strong-willed and stubborn. They detach and retreat when things are imbalanced or quarrelsome. They would love to rely on others, especially when finances are concerned, and sometimes take on a victim role without realizing it. They hold grudges like an Olympic event and will avoid the compromise in a passive way. Despite not trusting, they have a hard time saying no. They allow others to push them and push them, then find their fiery side flare and push back with Libra venom. If you like to get in and out of a shopping mall, don't take this Libra with you. You'll likely see their indecisiveness throughout the trip, with a final choice in their hands, only to back out right at the cashier.

Libra of Second Decan: October 4–13
Ruled by Uranus.

Positive Energy Traits: The second Libra decan is deep. They are fascinated by the human mind and love to observe social interaction. They love to psychologically analyze everyone, from strangers to family members. They immerse themselves in higher learning, loving anything abstract. They prefer the solitude and silence rather than the noise. When you are a friend of this Libra, consider yourself special because they are very particular with who they allow in their world and are often guarded. They are loyal and trustworthy.

Negative Energy Traits: The second decan Libra is often consumed with feeling insecure. They often feel glum about their situation, whether negative or positive, and will wallow in feeling shortchanged rather than manifesting the best. This energy expects the worst. Stubborn and indecisive, this Libra is wishy-washy on any and every decision.

Libra of Third Decan: October 14–23
Ruled by Mercury.

Positive Energy Traits: The third decan Libra is the most imaginative of the three. They are charming and have an amazing gift of communication and persuasion. This Libra is often cynical and witty, but they make it look charming, nonetheless.

Always observant, logical, empathic, and intuitive, this energy has an inner lie detector built in. They also have the gift of reading people and acting accordingly. It's this trait that makes them wonderful managers—even though they may say they'd rather be a recluse and not deal with anyone. They really are quite outgoing and able to interact with different social circles comfortably.

Negative Energy Traits: The third decan of Libra can come across as fidgety and restless. Although they are incredibly loyal to friends and family, and even their career, they get bored easily. They need to multitask and use their many gifts to their advantage, but although they may pretend, they have worth in their capabilities; they are truly good pretenders. This strong energy is sometimes so strong they forget they can take their superhero cape off and rest, and that burnout is real and dangerous.

September Libra vs. October Libra

The September Libra is neat and orderly.

The October Libra is messy and disordered.

The September Libra loves to be coddled and taken care of.

The October Libra loves to be social, but also needs time to withdraw.

The September Libra gets their feelings hurt easily.

The October Libra is blasé and doesn't much care what others say and think.

The September Libra tells little white lies, often with drama
and exaggeration.

The October Libra is exactly who they show you they are.

The September Libra feels as if others owe them something.

The October Libra works hard to have what they have.

The September Libra holds grudges.

The October Libra gets upset but gives several chances.

The September Libra will forgive but won't ever forget.

The October Libra needs balanced relationships and will
make changes if necessary.

Libra Masculine and Feminine Energy

Energy has a yin and yang that is interpreted as feminine and masculine, and according to the energy it is explained below:

Feminine September Libra: The feminine energy of a Libra in September is warm-hearted and loving. They are ambiguous in
all aspects of their life, which can sometimes make them look
naïve. This makes this Libra a follower rather than a leader.
They are hard workers but move at a slower, more precise
pace, and those who are high energy may see them as lazy.
A pushover, they often are talked into doing something they
aren't happy with but are afraid to voice their concerns. With
age and wisdom, this Libra finds strength and a bit more of a
voice. Finances are a lifelong struggle as they love their luxuri-
ous items, and they love to share whatever wealth they obtain.

Masculine September Libra: The masculine energy of a Libra in September will do whatever it takes to choose the middle road to
try to please everyone. They sometimes detach and withdraw
for fear of being put into a space where they must decide. They
have a salesperson spirit but decide it's easier to withdraw to

a cubicle. This Libra is warm, loving, and compassionate. They hate arguments and want intellectual conversation.

Feminine October Libra: The feminine energy of a Libra in October is sassy, witty, cynical, and intellectual. They love the finer arts, listening or playing music, being surrounded by books, and around anything and anyone creative. They can tackle challenging jobs and create an air of balance and diplomacy with grace. They love justice and fighting for those unable to fight for themselves. They have a healing energy toward humans and animals.

Masculine October Libra: The masculine energy of a Libra in October is sassy and intellectual. They love fine arts, listening or playing music, and anything and anyone creative. This Libra is often seen as shallow, incorrigible, and unreliable. They put on an air so as not to seem transparent or vulnerable. This Libra works very hard for their money but will often complain they aren't earning enough.

Libra Positive Traits

Peacekeeper

Libras aren't fans of conflict (unless they've created it). They are social creatures and will bend over backward to make others happy and feel included. Libras are sensitive to energy. Negativity exhausts them, so they will do whatever it takes to keep the energy balanced, sometimes at the sacrifice of their happiness.

Creative

Even if a Libra doesn't feel creative, they ooze a creative vibe and love surrounding themselves with all things artistic. If the Libra can incorporate something creative into their life, they will be at their happiest. It might be music, meditation or yoga, books, painting, jewelry making, or creative management or anything and everything in between. They love socializing, speaking, teaching, and learning.

Intuitive

While everyone has their own intuitiveness, the Libra's intuition is super special and intense. It could be because they don't like to conform to what society tries to tell them to be. It's that lack of restriction that heightens the intuition from a whisper to a roar. The Libra is a master manifester for themselves and helps enable the same in those they love. Libras are sensitive and very psychic, throwing a deck of Tarot cards out on their desk to see how they should be guided and in what ways.

Libra Negative Traits

Doesn't Compromise

In a Libra's world there should always be a compromise. Whether in business or romance, a Libra often sacrifices themselves waiting for someone else to swoop in and create the balance. You will start to see the Libra flail when the superhero doesn't show up. This can cause depression and arguments.

Indecisive

Libras can be perceived as lazy and absent-minded. It's because they can take forever to make any decision—from what jeans to buy to what canned soup to make. The larger the decision, the larger the indecisiveness. The sign of scales, Libras are constantly weighing their options, worried once they've decided their final decision might be wrong. Then they concern themselves with the what-if consequences.

Grudges

Libras are known to hold grudges against people as a knee-jerk reaction for being hurt. Libras want to trust and are incredibly sensitive. They care. They care about harmony. They want to be forgiving. But if there's no change to a situation and they are the only one carrying the weight, they will passively step away and they will avoid. They will carry the grudge without even telling the other party what the root of the problem is or giving them the ability to fix it. They will sometimes forgive, but they will never forget.

Libra Keywords

Libra Communication Style

Libras are colorful and creative, and like the communication to be interesting, social, and intellectual. Have patience with the Libra as they figure out how to form their words and they learn how to trust and share their thoughts and beliefs.

Libra Misconceptions

Libra is by nature the peacemaker. Although they rarely lose their calm, they are passionate and intense. Don't underestimate a Libra. They love harmony and diplomacy, and if they see someone being hurt by lack of balance, watch out—the sweet and charismatic Libra will show another side you don't want to be on.

Don't Be a Libra, Libra

Libra, you can be fun-loving, charming, and intelligent, but when you go into your dark place, watch out. You certainly know how to break a heart. You also are the queen/king of avoidance, especially when it comes to confrontations. The real lesson for you, Libra, is to know it's okay to speak up for yourself. You are loved, so stop faking it, start faithing it.

Thoughts from a Libra

The Devil's Advocate

Many Libras believe they have the most difficult experience because they are the Libra. Always second-guessing themselves. Always being hurt by others because they are so trusting and so loyal. Always taking care of everyone else but themselves.

> "Being a Libra can be difficult, mostly for others. For me, it is a daily struggle not to play devil's advocate with every single situation that may arise. I'm also very trusting and loyal. Too trusting and loyal sometimes. I find that if I give you my trust and loyalty and you break it, it is unforgivable and unforgettable. I have to work hard on forgiving those who've hurt me, more so for myself

than anyone else. I also have a hair-trigger temper, but that is usually brought on by high levels of anxiety—probably because I find, as a Libra, I am quite empathic and when everyone's emotions are tossed into the mix it can be hard to keep my cool. Like the scales of the Libra, I find that there are equal positive and negative sides to my sign, but I think if I were to change too much about myself, I'd then become unbalanced."

—Christy

Scales of Justice

Libras don't like a tipping scale and would prefer it balanced exactly the way they see fit.

"What most people don't realize about Libras is that we value fairness, justice, and balance most of all. All my life I have stood up for the underdog, even when it wasn't my fight to fight. I can't stand seeing injustice in the world, and although I am usually happy-go-lucky, I want harmony and hate arguing. Nothing makes me move toward a fight faster than an unfair situation. Be careful when dealing with a Libra if you like drama and conflict. They will avoid it and appease you just to keep things harmonious until the time that an injustice occurs. Then be ready for the gloves to come off and for them to head straight for your jugular."

—Leslie

Balancing Act

Libras truly want everything in their life balanced just so, including the home and surroundings.

"I was born under the sign of Libra. I've always heard it stood for balance. I guess this explains why I'm more or less OCD about everything. Pictures must be even on the walls and things have to be the same on one side as the other. It gets so bad that I have walk into a stranger's house and straighten pictures on their walls. Everything I do seems to prove that I am a typical Libra in some ways."

—Becky

Libra and Relationships

Strengths

Libras are very enthusiastic and open for adventures. They care deeply, are quick-witted, and love to make others happy. They love to feel safe and secure, and will offer the same, above and beyond, toward their partner. Even with flaws, they have a gentle way of overlooking them and seeing the best in their partnership. They are charming and supportive of their partner's endeavors, sticking up for their family, friends, and love relationships. They are nice, but they aren't stupid, so don't test their solidarity or patience.

Challenges

The Libra sees what they want, and they know how they want it, but they don't know how to communicate the big picture. It's scary to be vulnerable for them to simply vocalize their needs and so they hee and haw, sometimes looking like a deer in headlights. Because they are intuitive, they expect everyone else to be mind readers. Libras do love to argue and won't let up until their partners give in—it's why Libras make amazing attorneys.

Libra in the Workplace

Strengths

Libras love fairness and flourish best with an atmosphere of rules and regulations, justice, and clear judgment. A Libra boss won't play favorites and will be trustworthy and honest. They truly want you to succeed. They love to socialize and will act more like a peer rather than a superior, trying to make everyone happy.

Challenges

The Libra boss is a pushover that is indecisive and hates making decisions, all the while pretending they have it all together. Time management isn't their best trait, as they procrastinate and do everything methodically. This can be particularly frustrating for the employee who is under pressure on a project.

Parenting a Libra Child

A Libra child does get mad. They get angry. But they often show it when retreating. Stay in tune to your child and their emotions. Allow them the space and time to sort it out but be close for a shoulder to cry on and some help with resolving the conflict with love and understanding. You may not hear the whole story, and don't pressure them.

Strengths

Creative: The Libra child likes life to be as creative as possible. Give them a book, a movie to watch, music to play, and an environment to creatively flourish in, and you will see them soar.

Peacekeeper: If there's conflict, this Libra will try to mediate it as well as they can. The Libra child can see the right and the wrong, and they try to make it as right as possible.

Social: Did you say there's a birthday party to go to? The Libra child will likely be invited to several and will flourish with their charm and sweetness. Your Libra child is a social butterfly, and even though they may pretend they don't want to be the center of attention, somehow they always are.

Sensitive: The Libra child feels everything. They feel their family member's sadness and their joy, their fear, and their happiness.

Challenges

Indecisiveness: It takes a lot of patience to parent a Libra because they are wishy-washy. They like to carefully weigh their options, and then reconsider. Trying to rush them into a decision will only make them grumpy and even more indecisive.

Time Issues: It takes a lot of patience to parent a Libra. Sound familiar? Because of the indecisiveness they don't do well being hurried. They need thought-out organization and an understanding that it's part of who they are. Sometimes, though, their time issues look lazy and passive.

Generous: Libras will happily hand over their lunch to someone who forgot theirs. They love to help others and be there for everyone who needs them. They love harmony and balance, sometimes at their own sacrifice.

Sensitively Sick: The Libra child feels the energy of others and it can physically make them ill. If your child is detaching, you might want to look at your environment. Is there more worrying or arguing, an illness, or another imbalance? If there is, your Libra could complain of mysterious illnesses that could manifest into a true and real illness.

Parenting the Parent: The Libra wants to be treated as a peer rather than a child, and the parent can forget the appropriate roles.

The grown-up Libra child can become resentful for lack of a childhood.

Libra as a Parent

Strengths

Social: The Libra parent will sign their child up for every activity, and then be a pushover and let their child quit when they become bored. They love to throw and attend social functions.

Creative: The Libra parent will cart their child to the symphony, karate, and hit concert. They'll help their child paint and decorate their room several times over, and Pinterest as many amazing creative ideas for future birthday cakes or a wedding twenty years yet to come.

Negotiator: Libras hate tension and imbalance, so they do their best to negotiate and calm the choppy waters. They teach compromise and generosity.

Advisor: The Libra is an amazing advisor, with wisdom and love. They do a great job with seeing and sharing the insight with others (not always for themselves).

Challenges

Sarcastic: Sarcastic? A Libra? No, not a Libra?! It's just part of their wiring, and they don't realize it can come across as mean and critical.

Time Issues: Your Libra parent will be late for events big and small, wondering why anyone is even upset. The party starts when they show up, after all.

Financial Issues: Libras go through financial issues because they want to make their kids happy with the newest and the best, at the expense of opening their wallets wide.

Sensitively Sick: The Libra parent feels the energy of others, which can make them physically ill with mysterious illnesses that could manifest into a true and real illness.

Pushover: Ice cream for dinner? A note to get out of school and then a trip to the amusement park? Oh, you have a tummy ache and want to skip exams? This Libra parent can be the biggest pushover, wanting so much to stay in the good graces of their child, they forget to be an authority figure.

Libra and Finances

Libras really do want a balanced bank account, but they often get bogged down with all the decisions that money brings. Indecisiveness in the category of finances can bring anxiety and depression. The Libra needs someone to help teach, manage, and balance them to give them confidence.

Moon in Libra

The Libra moon energy draws your attention to the fairness or injustice in all aspects of your life. It urges you to look at ways you can help bring in more balance in your life (New Moon) or how to rid yourself of what isn't helping you with your balance (Full Moon).

Emotions are intensified in the Libra energy and you will feel urged to find harmony and balance in your life. You may feel braver than you have in a long time. This is the time to take thought-out chances and risks that will help you create more independence in your life. Remember that thoughts create things, so even making slight changes to how you think about what you want and how you want it (leave a deadline date out of it), can plant the seeds to new beginnings. The intensified emotions, however, are your battle song. You can hear the "I'm not good enough" in the wind of energy, or you can battle through and make the shift to "I've always been good enough and things are getting better." Don't be afraid, just believe.

New Moon in Libra

During this time, you'll feel a need for fairness and justice, but that isn't always life, right? If someone cuts you off in traffic, instead of taking matters in your own hands, just let it go. You will want to be an enforcer, but it isn't needed—allow the Universe to do it instead. Especially watch your sarcasm and cynicism as it rarely helps in any situation, so be careful of your mood and your mouth. There are karmic lessons that you will be showered with this moon that will teach you to be assertive and in control.

This Energy in Libra is Great for:

Looking at your sense-of-life balance. What is making you feel "off"?

Making an appointment with a doctor or dentist for your annual physical.

Having some one-on-one honest and loving time with your partner.

Full Moon in Libra

This unpredictable energy could make you feel off-kilter and out of control with life. Full moons are mirrors to our souls, and this moon is about wanting peace, love, and harmony in all aspects of life and yet feeling like we are on a teeter-totter. Look at the things that are causing this and look at ways you can correct this.

Full moons are also about endings. You might see an ending of a job or of a relationship/friendship. But once again, with endings come new beginnings. Say with the ending of a job, it could also mean a promotion, not exactly the unemployment line. There will more than likely be difficult weather patterns, issues with other countries, and disturbing headlines. Oddly enough, though, you won't want to create drama even though it will circle around you. As the moon is in Libra, you will crave justice in situations gone wrong and not everybody will see eye to eye. Libra often holds grudges and keeps it contained. Past issues become present issues, but it might be called something new.

This moon is not about being a martyr and allowing everybody else to distract you; instead, the next few days are about focus and building your life and taking steps toward your dreams and aspirations.

Soul Work

Libra energy is about creating balance in your life. List five things you want more of in your life, and then list five things you want less of in your life. How will you feel is your life is more balanced? How much can you control with creating more balance?

Create a visualization for what your most balanced life looks like. Here are some examples:

> If I organize my clothes by days, I will make time in the morning to do a five-minute meditation.
> If I make breakfast and lunches for the kids the night before, it will make for a calmer morning.
> If I go grocery shopping at lunch hours on Wednesdays, I have an extra hour to run to the gym.

Achieving life balance isn't complicated, it just takes some soul searching.

Now Is the Time

Do be careful to not get involved in the drama or act as a mediator. Not right now. Don't get involved with those who throw you their neediness. Do be lovingly assertive. Don't get engaged in the drama. Do talk to yourself lovingly. Don't speak without thinking first. It's a time of misconstrued communication.

Libra Totem Animal

Raven

The Libra energy embraces the raven totem, which focuses on intuition and creativity. The raven is known for being intelligent, but they are the worst secret keepers, sharing their treasure finds with just one caw. They show themselves to others as mysterious with a deep introspect. They balance the dark with the light, show off their social side, and share their magical and healing gifts.

The raven offers a gift of:

Introspection

Courage

Creativity

Magic

Healing

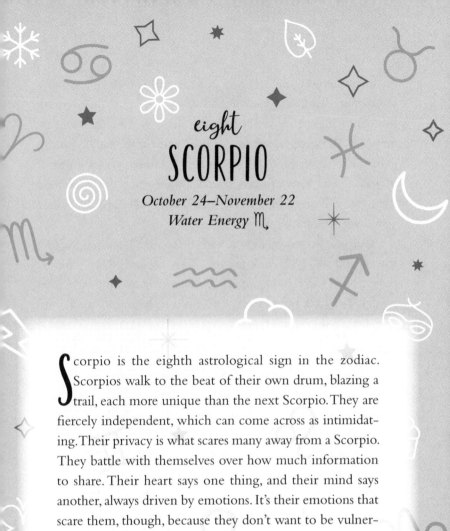

eight
SCORPIO

October 24–November 22
Water Energy ♏

Scorpio is the eighth astrological sign in the zodiac. Scorpios walk to the beat of their own drum, blazing a trail, each more unique than the next Scorpio. They are fiercely independent, which can come across as intimidating. Their privacy is what scares many away from a Scorpio. They battle with themselves over how much information to share. Their heart says one thing, and their mind says another, always driven by emotions. It's their emotions that scare them, though, because they don't want to be vulnerable, and yet they don't want to be guarded. The Scorpio will look around at their prey: I mean look around to see the people around and feel out the environment. It's then that the Scorpio will make a recommendation to themselves on what part to play. It's why some can describe the same person so differently.

If you can gain the attention of a Scorpio, you should consider yourself special. They don't like to waste their time on anything less than authentic, so don't toy with them because they will always win the game. Scorpios are loyal and passionate. If you can gain the trust of the Scorpio enough for them to come out of their shell, you have a forever friend. Unless you betray them, and then you will meet your worst enemy who will burn the bridge and never look back.

Scorpios are very generous with their time. They are problem solvers and will go to task for you. They do everything with intensity and with a big heart. They love hard and they fight even harder. They get bored easily and need to be entertained, until they decide they don't.

Scorpio Decans

Each zodiac is broken down into triplicities, each having their own energy added to their zodiac sign. This is Scorpio broken down:

Scorpio of First Decan: October 24–November 2
Ruled by Pluto and Mars.

Positive Energy Traits: This Scorpio is intense and driven, cool and collected. When life kicks them down, they brush it off, rebound, and start anew. This energy isn't afraid of new beginnings and is very courageous. They love the creative arts, as it soothes the monsters in their mind. They also love the romance of life itself.

Negative Energy Traits: This Scorpio likes privacy, which can be a lonely place. They are their own worst enemy with obsessive behaviors, depression, and deep grief.

Scorpio of Second Decan: November 3–12
Ruled by Neptune.

Positive Energy Traits: This Scorpio loves the mysterious. They are unafraid of the darker side, interested in the mystical and the occult. They are always searching for their purpose, a positive and negative trait. They rarely see life at face value, digging deeper, looking for hidden meanings. This Scorpio has a big heart, and if you are playing the game by their rules, you'll survive just fine.

Negative Energy Traits: This Scorpio can be manipulative and conniving. They say they want peace, harmony, and love, but they also create the drama that upsets the very thing they say they want. If you upset them, they will cut you off without looking back. Always charismatic, they like to look sweet with hints of dark shadows.

Scorpio of Third Decan: November 13–22
Ruled by the Moon.

Positive Energy Traits: This Scorpio is determined to embrace their inner power and strengthen through research, knowledge, intuition, and self-reflection. They give of themselves freely, taking care of the ones they love, sometimes in a sacrificial way. Wonderful managers and problem solvers, they try to trust their intuition while they walk their life path.

Negative Energy Traits: This Scorpio has a deep emotional language. When they are sad, they are at their lowest. When they are happy, they are at their highest, and there's rarely a middle ground. They see the worst and then the best in a matter of moments. They never forget, and they can be vengeful.

October Scorpio vs. November Scorpio

Along with each sign being split into their third decans, there is a difference between each zodiac split between the months.

October Scorpio comes across as cold.

November Scorpio has a hard time
controlling their emotions.

October Scorpio is a deep thinker.

November Scorpio is a deep thinker
and is also a communicator.

October Scorpio deflects emotions.

November Scorpio is social.

October Scorpio is helpful and considerate.

November Scorpio is helpful and takes over.

October Scorpio is persuasive.

November Scorpio connives until someone gives in.

October Scorpio doesn't want to be bothered.

November Scorpio is inquisitive.

October Scorpio loves to be romanced.

November Scorpio loves to romance.

October Scorpio is resentful.

November Scorpio is stubborn.

Scorpio Masculine and Feminine Energy

Energy has a yin and yang that is interpreted as feminine and masculine, and according to the energy it is explained below:

Feminine October Scorpio: The feminine energy of a Scorpio in October is a deep feeler, hidden within sarcasm and melancholy. They have an amazing ability to survive and overcome odds thrown at them. Passionate and mindful, this Scorpio needs to delve into a creative purpose—the arts, music, exercise, writing, and so on. They are prone to depression and addictions if they don't keep their body, mind, or soul occupied. Because of this they are looked at as the lesser Scorpio, not as strong and confident as their November sisters and brothers. This Scorpio energy simply wants to be accepted and to belong, but they instead feel left out. Sarcastic and bitter, funny and complex, this energy loves to be loved and needs to be reminded how wonderful they are in order to keep them on track. Handle them with care, though, because they do have the Scorpio stinger and will lash out when you don't expect it.

Masculine October Scorpio: The masculine energy of a Scorpio in October is sexy and complicated, obsessive and jealous. This energy often comes across as not wanting to make a commitment or set firm plans, but there's a sensitivity and a longing to be needed behind the tough exterior. This Scorpio may disappear and reappear, wondering why anyone got mad. A lot of excuses of being too busy and pulled into too many directions is often used. It's about firming up priorities and allowing the vulnerabilities to come through that is a lifelong lesson for this energy, and anyone who has a masculine October Scorpio in their life will have to be patient and forgiving many times over. This energy is always right, according to them. They are the smartest of all, according to them. And you should just be glad you are in their presence, according to them. When they let that macho and smart-mouthed act down, you'll find a smart, funny, and interesting person who has lots of ideas and lots of fears.

Feminine November Scorpio: The feminine energy of a Scorpio in November is charismatic and charming. Not only do they want to accomplish their own goals, but they want to help others with theirs. As much as this Scorpio portrays themselves as confident and driven, they are quite tenderhearted, afraid of being hurt or criticized. They are quiet worriers that swing between concern about finances and concern about family and friends. With finances, they figure it out like a champ even when they are at their lowest. With family and friends, they want to solve problems for them. Then the pendulum swings over to a concern of if they are truly pursuing something that will leave a legacy. Caring, domesticated, and enchanting, this energy has a special circle of friends and family, yet often feels unloved and unworthy and is tirelessly in pursuit of accomplishments in order to conjure a moment of success, only to be on the go yet again, always their own worst enemy. Betray this Scorp and it's remembered forever.

Masculine November Scorpio: The masculine energy of a Scorpio in November is strong, silent, and sexy. This energy loves fiercely, and is loyal, independent, and deeply passionate. It's hard to get a good read or first impression of a November masculine energy as they like to present themselves as mysterious and protected. This Scorpio is self-made, with ideas and fortitude to accomplish what they set out to do. Sometimes it stops at the ideas and they can quickly turn lazy and point fingers at others as to why the success didn't happen, calling out excuses of treason and sabotage. This energy will have half-done projects, quickly get bored, and move on to the next exciting idea only to start all over again. Moody and hot-tempered, you may only see a flicker of the eyes to shifting emotions, but the wrongs turn to hurtfulness that is kept stored in the memory forever.

Scorpio Positive Traits

Intuitive
If you ever need a lie detector machine, simply ask a Scorpio for a direct dial into intuition. Scorpios have a special insight, able to

embrace their supernatural guidance. Deep, mysterious, and hypnotic, the Scorpio can feel the environment and know if it's safe or not. It's a magical trait that Scorpios are very proud to have.

Determined

Scorpio is extremely passionate, focused, and determined. They love to take the lead, but if they aren't the boss, they will happily let the boss believe they are in charge. Scorpio is a wonderful problem solver with an ability to feel out their peers and competition.

Kindhearted

Although a Scorpio tries to keep their feelings hidden, they are extremely kindhearted. Scorpio knows the tragedy of life and wants to soften the ugly of the world to those they love. They do this with humor, thoughtfulness, and understanding. The Scorpio is protective of those they love. They are loyal and faithful, sometimes to a fault.

Scorpio Negative Traits

Jealous

Jealousy is a common theme for a Scorpio, and they are most known for carrying around the monster of green envy. The Scorpio has such deep emotions that they try to hide behind sarcasm and wittiness. They love deeply, and when it's not reciprocated it feels like intense betrayal. It's not so much what someone did to them to make them jealous either, but more of the insecurity that they aren't good enough to get the approval of the other person. It leads to depression, vengefulness, resentfulness, and anger, but it begins as jealousy.

Suspicious

Scorpios have trust issues even if there's no reason to be untrusting. Scorpios will check for faithfulness and loyalty on a constant basis, which is exhausting for the Scorp and exhausting for their friends, family, and partners. When wronged, they won't easily forgive and can bring it up years later as if it happened the day before.

Emotional

Scorpios feel so much more than any other zodiac sign. They love deeply. They fall hard. They are private, secretive, vengeful, and moody. They can turn melancholy and then turn to upbeat and the life of the party in a matter of moments.

Scorpio Keywords

Scorpio Communication Style

Scorpios love the language of seduction and mystery. They want you to vibe with them—look them in the eye. Tell them the truth. Don't give them fluff or fib. If you express your feelings to a Scorp, whether about music, pizza, or them, they will honor you. They want to be surrounded by interesting people. A Scorpio can be cynical, sarcastic, and opinionated. If you ask their opinion, you will hear the truth and it won't be covered in frosting. There is no mincing words with a Scorp. If they are feeling hurt, scared, or confused you will see the Scorp withdraw and seem distant. They brood and pout. Sometimes they do it to collect their thoughts. Sometimes they do it for drama. Sometimes they don't want to hurt anyone, so they distance themselves. So even if the Scorp isn't talking, they are always listening.

Scorpio Misconceptions

Scorpios have a reputation for being extremely sexual. It's not that they aren't, because they are, but it's more about feeling a connection to the other person rather than the act. A Scorpio is initially felt as icy cold. It's the sense of security that a Scorpio really wants and the fear of being disappointed that set the temperature. Once you're graced with the trust of a Scorpio, they thaw into something warm and loving. That connection to a Scorpio is a true exchange of energy of body, mind, and spirit.

Don't Be a Scorpio, Scorpio

Scorpio, you like to hide in the shadows with a mysterious allure. You watch, soaking in every word said. Ironically, you want everyone else to expose their souls, all the while staying secretive and embracing vengefulness. You love to own the unknown in your intense and manipulative way. Scorpio, your lesson is to realize you're intelligent and you don't need to be shady, cruel, or calculating. People will love you for being you.

Thoughts from a Scorpio

Just Love Me

Although Scorpios are guarded, they truly just want to be loved, preferably by someone who doesn't want to try to change them. They want someone who understands that they will probably never understand them and that's okay.

> "Having been born a Scorpio, I've become accustomed to the misconceptions that tend to be made for those of us born under this fantasizing astrological sign. Many people seem to think that Scorpios come off as aloof, stuck-up, or intimidating. While I can attest to the fact that my face can look unenthused in its resting phase, I am usually just observing my surroundings while deep in thought. Outsiders may also have a hard time breaking through a Scorpio's hard shell; once someone has betrayed our trust or love, it is hard for us to tear down that wall we have built. However, once we emerge and open up to a soul that we find trustworthy enough, it will be easy to see that, deep down, Scorpios are just big softies filled with a lot of emotions and love for those close to us. While Scorpios have plenty of negative traits associated with them, we also have several positive traits. We are thoughtful, caring, giving, good listeners, understanding, and willing to speak up for those who cannot

defend themselves. Scorpios love deeply and are fiercely loyal to the people we have personal relationships with, and when given the chance, you will see that Scorpios are not as scary as they can seem to be!"

—Katie

Blessing and Curse

There is hardly a middle ground when it comes to a Scorpio. It's either this or it's that, both of which are at intense levels.

"Being a Scorpio is both a blessing and a curse. When we love, we love and when we hurt, we hurt. We feel things to the extreme, so romance is always full of passion, we wear our heart on our sleeve; we are private to the point of being considered secretive and our loyalty knows no bounds. That's not to say that when we're crossed or feel betrayed that the Scorpion stinger doesn't come out, and if we get to that point, the wrath can also be extreme. Just ask someone who's been on the receiving end. Sometimes being a Scorpio means being misunderstood, but for me, I embrace it and welcome the next adventure life is going to throw my way."

—Rebecca

I'm Pretty Cool, I Just Cry a Lot

Scorpios try to portray a tough-as-nails, take-no-prisoners attitude. The reality is Scorpios feel everything, and each individual Scorp deals with it differently. Some grow bitter. Some resentful. Some embrace it.

"'You're way too sensitive,' he told me. 'If you were only stronger. If you had thicker skin. If you were ...' 'Someone other than me,' I replied with tears rolling down my cheek. The same tears that angered him. The same tears that made him think I was weak. The fact was, I felt everything. I still do. I feel the lies. I feel the broken promises. I feel the hurt. I feel the grief. I feel everything, and always have. It takes a lot for someone to feel everything and to not disappear in the hurt of it all. Scorpios try to come across as solid as possible, but the reality is we are mushy—we just don't want anyone to see that. It's because of our fear of vulnerability that we put up walls of coldness and that often makes us look like total jerks. Behind the act, we are the biggest feelers. If you take patience to see that, you'll have an amazing and loyal friend. Just know, though, we do cry a lot—sad, happy, mad, and just because."

—Kristy

Scorpio and Relationships

Strengths

A Scorpio loves harder and longer, and fights for that love harder and longer than any other sign. They are loyal and faithful in relationships, although they do get into trouble for being flirty. A Scorpio truly believes in forever when you finally get them to say it. They are romantic and love to be romanced. They are passionate and want to surrender to love, it just takes them a bit to admit it to the one they love—ever cautious.

Challenges

The Scorpio has a reputation for being secretive and yet smothering, jealous, and aloof. They say they aren't into you, but they are so into you in an obsessive way. Cautious at first then planning a wedding the next moment. It's intense, with both highs and lows. The Scorpio doesn't trust easily and will set up a series of quests to see if their potential mate will succeed at winning their love.

Scorpio in the Workplace

Strengths

Scorpios want the best of the best out of themselves, the business, and their employees. If you utilize your talents and gifts, the boss will happily reciprocate with praise and raises. The Scorpio boss won't micromanage if you do your job and you do your job well. If you set your ego down, act gentle and loving, and you are empathic with clients, peers, and your boss, then you will flourish with a Scorpio boss. They truly want to help you shine and succeed, so just do your job, try not to bother them too much, follow the rules, and keep your nose clean.

Challenges

The Scorpio boss holds grudges and never, ever forgets, especially if an employee is being sneaky or lying. The Scorp boss can be complicated and intense, moody and melancholy. They let their personal life dictate their daily mood and rarely want to divulge. If you can gauge their mood and tiptoe instead of instigating, life will be much easier. Also, if you have a question for your Scorp boss and you see they are busy, focused on something and your question can wait—then wait. Otherwise, you may see some claws come out and some heated snarkiness.

Parenting a Scorpio Child

The Scorpio child is their own person and they want to be treated in their own uniqueness, especially if there are other siblings. Don't compare or suggest they be more like this person or that person; instead, compliment and reward them for the gifts and talents they do have. They don't want to be changed, and they certainly don't need their insecurity to be fed; they beat themselves up enough.

Strengths

Intuitive: Don't be surprised if your Scorpio child has so-called imaginary friends—aka talks to those on the other side or to ghosts. Don't make fun of or tease them on this. They flourish with understanding.

Empathic: The Scorpio child is very in tune to what others are feeling and acts accordingly. If they sense tension around a parent, they may retreat. If they sense someone needs a hug, they will oblige.

Creative: The Scorpio child likes to embrace their creative side and will try out new opportunities until they find their gift. Let them try, succeed, and fail accordingly.

Loves People: Scorpios do like to be around people, the happier and more positive the better for the Scorp child. Arrange play-dates and know that the Scorp child will want to hang out with adults as well.

Loves to Learn: The Scorpio child loves to learn. They love to read, research, and dig. It doesn't necessarily mean they love school, though.

Challenges

Emotional: Some parents will call their child stubborn; however, the Scorpio doesn't see it that way. They simply feel everything and often feel as if they aren't understood. It's then you will see what it looks like to be stubborn.

Defensive: Any line of questioning, whether there's anything to hide or not, the Scorpio child will get defensive and snappy.

Sensitive: The Scorpio is very sensitive and will often retreat into a quiet place. Allow them to process their feelings without pushing or pressing. Give them space. They'll come out of their shell and communicate when they're ready.

Sneaky: Although Scorpios don't like anyone being sneaky, it's probably because they feel nobody can do it better than they do. They are suspicious, like to know what's going on, and want to be included. If that doesn't happen, they will dig for the scoop.

Scorpio as a Parent

Strengths

Observant: The Scorpio parent sees everything and hears everything, communicated and preserved with their sixth sense. They can gauge what their child's needs are accordingly.

Council: A Scorpio parent will gladly be their child's adviser along with parenting. They love to be asked for help—whether baking cookies for the wrestling tournament or love advice. Just make sure not to do it at the last minute or when they are focused on another project.

Protective: The Scorpio parent cares about their child(ren) and will defend them fervently. The shielding can come across as possessive, but it's all done in love.

Strong: No matter what type of life a Scorpio has, they dust themselves off and keep going. The Scorpio parent is a role model for perseverance.

Challenges

Ruler of the House: The Scorpio parent is certainly the ruler of the house. This can lead to power struggles with everyone in the house. The Scorp doesn't try to control out of mere ego, but more because they believe they are intuitive enough to know how the house should run.

Emotional: The Scorpio parent is moody. If work was difficult, they'll bring it home. If they are upset with a spouse, their mood will shift to negative. They may even project that anger out to their child. Example: If their boss yelled at them at work earlier, they will yell at their child about their room mess.

Alone Time: The Scorpio parent needs their self-care time or else they get snappy and sarcastic and will withdraw. A sensitive child may take this personally, when it has nothing to do with parenting but healing their soul.

Resentful: Did the child's best friend hurt their child? Or did the mom in PTA say something nasty about them or their child? Well, watch out, because the grudge is real, and the Scorpio's resentment isn't to be messed with.

Scorpio and Finances

Scorpios are conservative when it comes to money but when they do spend it, they know just the right investments to make, listening closely to their intuition. They are also generous and giving. But they are sensible: They like having cash in their pocket and a great credit score. If those go awry, it will be a big point of stress. Reliability and stability are everything to a Scorpio.

Moon in Scorpio

The Scorpio moon tends to be suspicious of the intentions of others, when they are both positive and negative. Nighttime dreams and your intuition will be intense during this time. Know that there are clues and cues to be discovered within.

New Moon in Scorpio

Scorpio often feels the edgy energy, sensing the tension and experiencing a heightened intuition and even seeing spirits or witnessing paranormal activity (sensing, smelling, feeling watched, etc.). This watery sign is super sensitive and super aware.

The Scorp energy gives you special *spidey senses* and so for the next few days you should be feeling quite psychic and intuitive, which means that nobody will be able to get away with anything as your gut instincts are turned all the way UP. This can draw some heightened emotions, so be cautious with being overdramatic, especially when it comes to love (or lack of love). You might be feeling overconfident and testy, so be careful bringing up issues suppressed for some time in both relationships and work. Instead, spend time writing down what's bothering you and looking at it when emotions may not be as raw.

This is a powerful sign. Know that you can harness the magic from the moon by asking for a promotion (in a tactful way), expressing your love, embracing your sexiness, and coming to terms with your emotional vulnerability, which can be used for good or for bad, as Scorpio energy has a means of bringing the stinger out and wanting revenge. Choose wisely.

Things to Do during This Time:
Soul search.
Light a candle.
Eat a good meal.
Drink lots of water.
Evaluate changes in your life.
Take action to make those changes a reality.

This New Moon helps shed what it isn't working and birthing some new opportunities.

Full Moon in Scorpio
Full Moons act as a mirror to your soul. It is as if all the emotional junk that you thought you had buried in the attic and the basement and had thrown in your emotional trunk has resurfaced. Those who have already done the emotional work will find Full Moons easy and comfortable. But those still hiding from themselves and their past might feel emotional and sad.

Sometimes you aren't even aware that there is still sludge left over from the past until a Full Moon arises and makes you look. Maybe you were avoiding on purpose or maybe you became so used to avoiding; no matter, this is a wonderful time for you to clean out the emotional soul clutter and de-junk.

This is a great time for you to look over your New Moon wishes and reaffirm what you want and throw away what you don't! It's time to burn your wishes from the past and trust that the Universe is taking care of them, and you don't have to hold on to fear like a baby blanket.

Things to Do during This Time:

> Climb into comfy pajamas.
> Snuggle with a significant other.
> Pour yourself a cup of coffee or tea.
> Grab a journal and do some soul searching.

Instead of beating yourself up for the stagnancy in life, or the steps backward, look at how to move forward.

Soul Work

Scorpio energy can be macabre and intuitive. The energy makes you dig into the inner psyche. This exercise helps to clarify what truly matters and what regrets and resentments you may be hanging on to.

Envision this as your last day on earth and ask yourself these questions:

> What am holding on to that's made me feel miserable?
> Who have I been angry with? I may have said I forgave, but I've held on to it.
> Does it really matter at this point, today, my last day on earth?
> Now write your obituary. What are your accomplishments? Who is listed as family and friends?

Take this information forward to see what really matters.

Now Is the Time

Do turn on the music and have a dance party. Don't dig into the emotional trunk of the past. Do embrace your unique self. Don't believe there's nobody to trust—there is. Do trust your intuition, even the little whispers and your nighttime dreams. Don't over-analyze and over-worry. Do keep away from the black cloud of depression. Don't channel your inner bitchiness.

Scorpio Totem Animal

Snake

Snakes are often feared, and yet hold an air of mystery, sometimes even seductive and unpredictable. Sounds like a Scorpio, doesn't it? The Scorpio, much like the snake, is busy reinventing themselves throughout their lifetime. The snake is misunderstood, and the Scorpio often feels the same. The snake wants to be social, but they also want everyone to know that when they are done, they are done. If you dare mess with them, they will strike with a powerful vengefulness, and you do have to be cautious around them just in case.

The snake offers a gift of:

Mystery

Change

Healing

Decisiveness

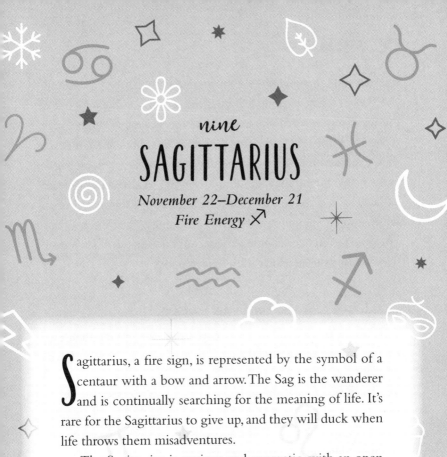

nine

SAGITTARIUS

November 22–December 21
Fire Energy ♐

Sagittarius, a fire sign, is represented by the symbol of a centaur with a bow and arrow. The Sag is the wanderer and is continually searching for the meaning of life. It's rare for the Sagittarius to give up, and they will duck when life throws them misadventures.

The Sagittarius is curious and energetic, with an open mind and enthusiasm to achieve their goals. They like to be in touch with what is going on in the world and will involve themselves in the world of others, but not in a busybody-type way. Although mostly extroverted, they hold a dual personality and are private with concerns of their own life. They like their freedom; don't question them if they withdraw into a moody and impatient fire-starter self.

Sagittarius is associated with the Archer, represented by an arrow. The Sagittarius looks for their target to shoot and focuses on that until they get their desires. They love to research and learn, and often get frustrated with themselves. If someone gets in their way, they will be ruthless to make them get out of the way. They can become cynical and can wallow in the negative, especially if they get bored and feel stuck. It's about the target and their exploration to get to where they want to. It's rare for a Sag to feel satisfied where they are, always wanting to adventure forward. Because of that you may find that the Sag changes their mind often, which can be frustrating for friends and family. They want to have stories to tell and constant experiences. It's not that they are indecisive; it's just that they don't want to feel stuck.

Sagittarius Decans

Each zodiac is broken down into triplicities, each having their own energy added to their zodiac sign. This is Sagittarius broken down:

Sagittarius of First Decan: November 23–December 2 Ruled by Jupiter.

Positive Energy Traits: This energy is filled with adventure and spirit. They love academia, research, and often make it their mission to be eternal learners and to share that information with intelligence and excitement. They are enthusiastic and their energy is contagious to those they meet. They will fight for justice and for something or someone they believe in.

Negative Energy Traits: This Sagittarius is highly competitive, which can come across as tactless, direct, and brash. Because they are intelligent, they don't have a lot of patience for those they believe aren't on their level.

Sagittarius of Second Decan: December 3–12
Ruled by Mars.

Positive Energy Traits: This Sagittarius is well-rounded with being intuitive, instinctual, and technically inclined. They are loyal, devoted, and kindhearted. They are the philosophers and deep thinkers. This Sagittarius needs a balance from being in their head by utilizing a physical outlet—whether yoga, dance, or a sport—to help this energy continue to feel structured.

Negative Energy Traits: This Sagittarius is headstrong and quickly loses interest. They can appear detached and push people away because they look and communicate like they aren't interested, when that may not be the case at all. They are fiercely independent and do well without being micromanaged, whether in work or in a relationship.

Sagittarius of Third Decan: December 13–21
Ruled by the Sun.

Positive Energy Traits: This Sagittarius has dynamic energy, is passionate and outgoing. They love to meet new people and have new experiences, drinking in adventure. This decan has integrity and is proud. They are trustworthy and are wonderful listeners.

Negative Energy Traits: This Sagittarius takes risks, makes rash decisions and can be impulsive. They often find themselves scrambling to climb out of the pitfalls they've created by not thinking things carefully through. They are the energy that quits their job with the ideal that something better is coming soon, and when it doesn't, they must crawl back to their old employer.

November Sagittarius vs. December Sagittarius

Along with each sign being split into their third decans, there is a difference between each zodiac split between the months.

November Sagittarius often stays in their shell until they can trust.

December Sagittarius is social and can talk to anyone and everyone.

November Sagittarius is often quiet and reserved.

December Sagittarius is energetic, extroverted, and bold.

November Sagittarius is introverted and thoughtful.

December Sagittarius is blunt, opinionated, and brash.

November Sagittarius is private regarding their own matters and others' matters.

December Sagittarius is private regarding their own matters.

Sagittarius Masculine and Feminine Energy

Energy has a yin and yang that is interpreted as feminine and masculine, and according to the energy it is explained below:

Feminine November Sagittarius: The feminine energy of a Sagittarius in November appears lighthearted and relaxed, but this energy has varying layers and is strong emotionally and spiritually. This energy is articulate, often going through the first half of life without being aware of their intellect or goal-setting. They find themselves—professionally and personally—through mere chance. They feel the need to control their situations so as not to feel they are putting others out, and they also don't want to sabotage or sacrifice their own limitations. This Sagittarius has sharp wit and an amazing sense of humor. People love to be around them and ask their advice.

Masculine November Sagittarius: The masculine energy of a Sagittarius in November is charming yet shy, and they are often afraid of making huge changes. With a bit of a dark side run rampant with insecurities and suspicions, they are heady with trying to sort out reality versus make-believe. This Sag does a great job of hiding their lack of worthiness by being progressive in their career and social life; they are a dream chaser.

Feminine December Sagittarius: The feminine energy of a Sagittarius in December is strong-willed and goal-oriented. Because of their determination they can achieve amazing things with their inner shine. Financially they do a wonderful job of budgeting. Sometimes unconventional, this energy can divulge their life story and the next moment zip up and act as if nobody really knows them. Some call it moody, they may call it private—it might be a little of both. This Sag wants the traditional family-like life but is afraid of being hurt and plays the boundary, pulling when the other pushes, and pushing when the other pulls. It's a lifetime of learning how to trust others, but most of all themselves.

Masculine December Sagittarius: The masculine energy of a Sagittarius in December is a natural scholar who loves to learn, teach, and have interesting conversations with anyone who might want to talk, or more likely, listen to them. This energy loves to research, plan, and dabble in different areas of learning. It's because this Sag has huge goals but sometimes puts too much on their plate; they overwhelm themselves with their constant thirst for knowledge and enthusiasm. This energy is shallow, gloating about what they've read, done, want to do, or might do.

Sagittarius Positive Traits

Straight Shooters

Sagittarians tell it like it is with harsh honesty. There's no mincing words or looking out for the fluffy feelings. They really don't care much if you share that your feelings are hurt either. If you can't take the heat, get out of the Sagittarian's world. It is refreshing, however, because the Sagittarius won't tell you what you want to hear but what you need to hear. They are a steadfast friend, as long as you can handle the truth.

Adventurous

If you want an experience, then the Sagittarius is your person to have it with. With their fearless nature and thirst for knowledge, passion, and optimism, they will take you off the beaten path even if just philosophically. The Sag loves to learn, play, and have fun and will try to find it even in everyday routines.

Natural-born Leader

The Sagittarius loves to blaze the path, and they aren't afraid to do it alone—no roadmap needed. They won't look for permission (sometimes this gets them into trouble) or approval. They know what they want and know what needs to be done and they do it. They aren't afraid to be by themselves, listening to their own thoughts, and taking time for self-care.

Sagittarius Negative Traits

Tactless

The Sagittarius doesn't love senseless drama but they often create it by being mouthy and opinionated. They don't care if you want to know what they are thinking; they will tell you anyhow, and it's often offensive and embarrassing. They believe honesty is the best policy, even if it hurts feelings.

Impatient

The Sagittarius is always on the go in body and mind, and all those in their world need to keep up. They can get easily bored, especially if they have to take on the role of follower, because they are natural leaders from birth. They know what they want, they want it now, and they want it the way they want it. They don't always play nicely.

Short-tempered

The Sagittarius is quick-tempered and a hot head. It's almost as if some days they wake up and spin an invisible wheel of *who should I be mad at today?* They become the target of the temper until the wheel is spun again and another victim is chosen. The temper comes fast and just as quickly disappears.

Sagittarius Keywords

Sagittarius Communication Style

Whether an introverted or an extroverted Sagittarian, they love to have true and real look-me-in-the-eyes type of conversations. Sagittarians have a tendency of over-promising and over-dramatizing, which can make those who know the ins and outs of their Sagittarian skeptical of what is said. They like the conversation to be upbeat and fun, sometimes philosophical, but be careful of making it too stressful or deep.

Sagittarius Misconceptions

Because a Sagittarius often detaches, it often comes across as being cold and hard. Sagittarians do like their space and their privacy, and they don't always know how to express themselves effectively. Once you get to know the ins and outs of the Sag's quirks, you see they are hardly cold; they are truly kind, caring, and loyal.

Don't Be a Sagittarius, Sagittarius

You're difficult, Sagittarius. You believe you know it all and it's hard to reason with your stubbornness. When was the last time you listened to someone else's opinions or views? When was the last time you listened to someone else's opinions or views and didn't criticize? Even when you're wrong, you will attempt to convince others and yourself how right you are. Sag, your lesson is to realize you aren't the only one hurt in your life and that sometimes it is you that is throwing cranky down and hurting the ones who love you.

Thoughts from a Sagittarius

Loyal and Loving

The Sagittarian is loyal and loving, and although they might complain and be blunt about your complaints of life situations, they will also be there to dry your tears and give you a hug, but also kick you in the rear to stop the whining.

> "Sagittarius people are known to be very loyal, dependable, and generous to a fault. We are not quick to judge and most likely we will forgive you repeatedly. Why? Because once you become a friend, we remain friends for life. If you can't hear the truth, then don't ask us a question. We are honest, blunt, and optimistic. I have a great sense of humor and am not afraid to take risks. If you want a relationship with a Sagittarius give her plenty of space and the freedom she craves. Because I am impulsive, I might be the one that calls you at 2:00 a.m. to plan to see a new movie or try a new restaurant. A lover of animals and the outdoors, you will always find me on a new adventure or traveling. I am the one you want to talk to if you need a positive outlook on life. The simple things in life make me happy! I can have a temper and I love a good argument, but after I cool down, I forget about what made me mad. You seldom can make me jealous or envious."
>
> —Vivian

The Traveler

The Sagittarian loves adventure, whether it's a cruise to Grand Turk or browsing a flea market on the weekend, or simply a glass of wine over dinner talking about life purpose.

> "I love challenges and I'm always up for them. Be it mental, physical, or emotional. I'm flexible, creative, and even a little bit of luck! I love to make people laugh, and can be eccentric, but it's all in fun. I love to learn about new things, places, and people. Traveling is my most happy time. Dream job, *National Geographic* photographer, or travel channel host like Samantha Brown."
>
> —Lisa

The Skeptic

Sagittarians will keep a filter up until they learn to trust. You have to earn a Sagittarian's loyalty and until you do, they may come across as a bit detached. Once you earn their allegiance, you'll have a Sag for life.

> "I have developed a sense of quiet before the storm. I tend to overthink and overreact. Most see me as aloof, but once the pretty bow is taken off, the onion layers are waiting. As a Sagittarius I am a skeptical person until I experience my skepticism in real life (as if that makes sense). Once I am comfortable in a situation, all bets are off. The 'filter' is lifted and it's on like Donkey Kong."
>
> —Ed

Sagittarius and Relationships

Strengths

Sagittarius relationships are intense and attentive. Once you win the trust and affection of your Sag you will find a loyal and openly communicative love. They are generous with their time and will keep you on your toes while they plan adventures. Most of all they will keep you laughing with their quick wit.

Challenges

Sagittarians work at a slow pace and need freedom and independence. They need to be careful and wait to make sure they can trust. They need to be assured there's security and a future. It's not that they have commitment issues; they simply put everything on pause, and then often in slow motion.

Sagittarius in the Workplace

Strengths

Sagittarians don't like to be bossed around, but they do like to be the boss, and they do make a great boss. Sag doesn't like to be micromanaged, and they carry that over in their leadership techniques and boss like they'd want to be bossed. They prefer to show their employees once and then watch them continue to learn in a hands-off type of way. They do best with employees who don't ask a lot of questions or distract them from their own projects.

Challenges

A Sagittarius boss isn't for the faint of heart. They are outspoken and frank, not afraid to call a spade a spade. They will unapologetically say the wrong thing at the wrong time or act unprofessional in the middle of a board meeting, and they won't understand what the big deal is.

Parenting a Sagittarius Child

Strengths

Sense of Humor: The Sagittarius child loves to laugh and will try to lighten the mood by making family and friends giggle, trying to keep the mood light.

Wisdom: Many Sagittarian children can be classified as old souls and have a wisdom beyond their years. They can just as happily hang with adults as they can children.

Optimistic: The Sagittarius child is happy, energetic, and charming. Because of this they have a large group of friends and will happily participate in various activities.

Challenges

Wild-Child: Don't be surprised if you find your little Sagittarian climbing the tree to care for baby birds or jumping into the deep end of the pool without a life jacket. They come into this world wanting adventure and they'll find it whether the parent wants it or not.

Rules? What Rules?: The Sagittarian child isn't a fan of rules and would rather create their own rules according to how they see things. They are happier being free-range raised. They feel stifled by rules and will push when you pull.

Blunt: It could be that "I'll wash your mouth out with soap" came from a parent of a Sagittarian. The Sag is sassy and says whatever they think and feel, even if it gets them into trouble.

Bored: The Sagittarius child needs to be entertained. Whether a visit to the mall or a drive to the lake, there must be an itinerary, at least until they decide they are good and go into reclusion.

Sagittarius as a Parent

Strengths

Playful: Sagittarian parents can be fun if they get out of their own head. They like to grab a suitcase and run to the airport or make a spontaneous day trip to the park or a baseball game. A Sag can turn anything into a fun and adventurous time.

Quickly Forgiving: The Sagittarius does have a quick temper, which is a negative, but they are quick to forgive and just as quick to forget. The Sag parent stays loyal and faithful despite arguments and disagreements.

Fun and Funny: The Sagittarius parent is serious when they need to be, but fun and funny with their children. They like to keep things light and loving.

Challenges

Unorganized: It's not that the Sagittarius is an Oscar the Grouch; it's that they are always on the go, rarely sitting still, that makes the priority to have everything in place not the priority.

Hurtful: The Sagittarius parent is outspoken and brash, witty and sarcastic. To a child it can come across as harsh and hurtful. When they get older, the child may see it as loving and helpful.

Temperamental: Mood swings are a constant in a Sagittarian's repertoire. Most of the time the moodiness has nothing to do with a person, but their own feelings of being frustrated, restless, or bored. However, the Sag is good for projecting their bad moods onto those close to them.

Sagittarius and Finances

The Sagittarius isn't necessarily into collecting things that money buys, but they do like to spend their money on experiences, especially if it involves travel and adventures. Later in life they often learn to save and plan for the future. They will likely beat themselves up for not doing it earlier. If they face a financial fallout, they quickly "adult" and figure out how to find financial freedom.

Moon in Sagittarius

The Sagittarius energy tackles the truths and perceived truths in life, uncovering and releasing, which can cause some heated and negative energy. The best thing to do is allow yourself to let it go and not fester in the energy of the argument.

New Moon in Sagittarius

Focus on positive things you want to create in your life. You won't always be liked. You won't always see eye to eye. And sometimes it's best to simply step away and not allow someone's dirt to get you dirty. You deserve to be loved, not ridiculed. You deserve to be supported, not hated on. Those who feel the need to be snarky, negative, or hateful in the name of whatever stance they are supporting now is not helping anything; they are only spreading more negativity. You have the choice to help spread that or to send them love, take the high road, and step away. A lack of boundaries invites disrespect. Love yourself enough to know when the waters are muddied so you can't see how deep it is and find yourself wondering why they aren't throwing you a life jacket.

What you may see during the Sagittarius New Moon phase:
> Anxious for an adventure.
>
> Finding that you're more vocal about your feelings—think foot-in-mouth moments.
>
> Traveling or scheduling travel.
>
> Exploring new perspectives and ideas.
>
> Meeting new people.
>
> Believing and following through on your flashes of intuition and insight.
>
> Staying optimistic and centered but not naïve.
>
> Buying stocks/investing.
>
> Taking a course on money.
>
> Writing a will.
>
> Figuring out financial issues with an expert.
>
> Adjusting the types of people you keep within your circle (including on social media).

Full Moon in Sagittarius

Frustration and impatience, two typical reactions to Full Moons, are both negative attributes, which throw more negativity your way. Turn off your negative mental chat that is sabotaging the life you so deserve. How do you do that? The first thing is by acknowledging that you are doing it and when a negative thought arises, tell yourself *STOP!* and replace the negative thought with a positive one. Or simply take some deep breaths. We can't always have a head full of sunshine, but little by little you will notice that your negative thoughts will start to dissipate. Think of it as mental scum and you are erasing it away with your happy thoughts. By simply turning down the volume of negative chatter, the things you have been wanting in your life will begin to show up—whatever you are dreaming of. Always remember that what you focus on expands, and if it is negative, then that is what you will get. Choose wisely. We are all being tested with the negative news and the negative energy.

Release your sadness (crying is a great release, as is working out) and reiterate your true wishes. You are the source of your thinking. You are the source of your behavior. There are no strings attached to you! You are the writer of your story. You make it happen. Watch your sass and your sarcasm. Trust your flashes of insight and maybe write them down, even if they sound silly. The Sag moon helps you take risks and release suppressed thoughts and people from your life. It's time to battle and believe.

Soul Work

The Sagittarian energy likes to pack up and go, which makes this energy great for clearing your space so you don't get weighed down. A simple and gentle way to clear energy and increase your well-meaning is to declutter your space. Take one drawer or one closet at a time and identify all your clutter. Clutter steals your joy and can cause anger, sadness, depression, and angst. Clutter is low and stagnant energy.

Label four boxes with: Keep, Donate, Throw Away, and Not Sure. The Keep box is obviously what you want to keep. The Donate box is given to friends, a charity, or sold. The Throw Away goes to the curb. The Not Sure box is to be marked on your calendar for six months in the future. If you haven't needed anything in the box in that time, give it away without opening it up and going through it again. Each day for ten to thirty minutes, choose a drawer or closet to go through. Pick up each item and put it in one of the boxes. Plan the time for your clutter-cleaning sessions. With every space you clear, you tell the Universe that you're ready for positive energy in your life.

Now Is the Time

Do embrace your inner wisdom. Don't be blunt, asking embarrassing questions and adding careless comments to conversations. Do book a trip or research a future adventure. Don't stay cooped up inside. Do be the life of the party. Don't go on a power trip. Do pick up a book or sign up for a class. Don't leap before making a pro/con list.

Sagittarius Totem Animal

Owl

The owl is known for its wisdom and insight, which is why the owl is a Sagittarian's totem. The Sag is the optimistic, enthusiastic, and wise adviser. The owl ventures in silence and independence, eye on the prize. The owl isn't afraid of charting through unfamiliar places to discover lessons and healings. Embracing the owl reminds the Sagittarius to see the big picture.

The owl offers a gift of:

Wisdom

Restless spirit

Keen insight

Reliable counsel

Optimism

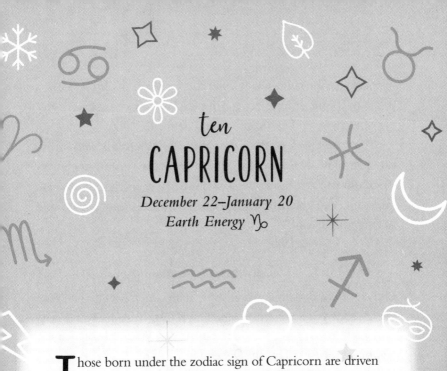

ten

CAPRICORN

December 22–January 20
Earth Energy ♑

T hose born under the zodiac sign of Capricorn are driven
and analytical. Being that a Capricorn is an earth sign, they
often see life with a cool head and are balanced through
and through. With a healthy mix of intuition and realism they
see through illusion and are hard-working and goal-oriented
in all aspects of life, whether it's a simple laundry day or a corporate meeting they are hosting.

Being that the Capricorn is an earth sign, grounded
and analytical, they are patient, calm, and handle pressure
well. A Capricorn is the one you want on your side during
an argument, and one you don't want against you in an
argument because even if you are in the right, they have a
way of proving that they are right.

Capricorns are often seen as reserved and guarded and
are very careful about whom they allow in their inner circle. Even if you've won their trust, you'll likely not see all

of them as they emotionally hold themselves back. If you need a problem solved or need advice, the Cap will be your person, giving objectivity and useful and sound council.

The Capricorn is often thought of as dull, stuffy, and sometimes shy, but they have a wonderful sense of humor once they clock out of their head, which is always busy solving the world's problems. The core of the Capricorn is sweet, funny, artistic, and filled with whimsy.

Capricorn Decans

Each zodiac is broken down into triplicities, each having their own energy added to their zodiac sign. This is Capricorn broken down:

Capricorn of First Decan: December 22–31
Ruled by Saturn.

Positive Energy Traits: This Capricorn is determined, but also patient with oneself and with others. They are wonderful friends and are amazing team members in their workplace. It's their practical, realistic, and tactful side that draws a crowd to them, always asking their opinion and advice.

Negative Energy Traits: This Capricorn is often seen as inflexible and rigid, mainly because they are so realistic. This isn't the Capricorn to sprinkle unicorns and make-believe fairytales at someone just to make them feel good. They are sensitive but practical.

Capricorn of Second Decan: January 1–10
Ruled by Venus.

Positive Energy Traits: This Capricorn is patient and relaxed. They still know how to accomplish their life goals. They are hardworking and sensitive to other people. This Cap is often creative and gifted in different facets of communication. This energy will set their own agendas aside to help friends and family.

Negative Energy Traits: The second decan of Capricorn is often obsessed with finances and although they like to travel and experience life, they also will have buyer's remorse and be moody as they see their bank account dip. It can make for some difficult relationship issues. If someone acts too nice around this Capricorn, they immediately conjure suspicions.

Capricorn of Third Decan: January 11–20
Ruled by Mercury.

Positive Energy Traits: This Capricorn is an amazing speaker and communicator. People are drawn to this energy because they have a practical intelligence and sound problem-solving skills. They are social when they want to be, turning on their charm and turning it off just as quickly.

Negative Energy Traits: This Capricorn is restless and impatient, sarcastic and witty. They are temperamental and overachievers, mainly due to being sensitive and wanting to see their worth show for something. Don't get in this Capricorn's way, though, or you will be cut with their words and their deep melancholy.

December Capricorn vs. January Capricorn

December Capricorns are practical with financial decisions.

January Capricorns see their worth through their bank account balance.

December Capricorns are patient, but if someone tries to abuse that, watch out.

January Capricorns won't tolerate stupidity and will call the person out on it.

December Capricorns are intuitively disciplined.

January Capricorns are intelligent.

December Capricorns get into their own head, overthinking and overanalyzing.

January Capricorns get into their own head and can become melancholy and depressed.

December Capricorns are rebellious.

January Capricorns are mysterious.

December Capricorns are negotiators.

January Capricorns don't really want to be bothered with stupidity.

Capricorn Masculine and Feminine Energy

Energy has a yin and yang that is interpreted as feminine and masculine, and according to the energy it is explained below:

Feminine December Capricorn: The feminine energy of a Capricorn in December is known for their stoic exterior personality. Their guardedness is a misunderstood fear of being vulnerable. You won't find this energy wearing their heart on their sleeve; it will take a bit to get close and gain their trust. This energy likes plans and then backup plans in case the main plan doesn't work. They take their work seriously, even if they don't find passion with what they're doing. Their poker face is often hard to determine if they are doing well or badly, though, and they like it that way.

Masculine December Capricorn: The masculine energy of a Capricorn in December is critical and overly practical. This energy builds high walls and if you can conquer all the obstacles on the quest over the wall, you'll find a sweet and loyal energy for life. It's not an easy quest, though. They may appear cold, unsympathetic, and unfeeling, yet they have a soft side and will wait patiently for the right one—a true closet romantic. This energy just wants stability in every part of their life.

Feminine January Capricorn: The feminine energy of a Capricorn in January is calculating and suspicious. Don't underestimate this energy. This Cap is intelligent, creative, serious, and focused. This energy is often their own worst enemy, even with all their gifts. They hide their insecurities with sarcasm and arrogance. Cross this Cap and you'll be met with a sharp tongue and unforgiveness. Stay in their charm and you'll find a loyal and classy energy that will protect you forever.

Masculine January Capricorn: The masculine energy of a Capricorn in January is moody. You must fit within their life and quirks because it will take a lot to convince them to change in order to fit within yours. This energy wants to be the priority, whether as a partner, employee, peer, friend, or parent. They are proud, stubborn, witty, and sarcastic. It's their ego that gets them into trouble, as often work life becomes the priority over personal life. They are goal-oriented and need constant accolades. This energy is open-minded, though, and loves to communicate (mostly about what they are doing), so make sure to stay truthful, but leave the criticism out of the conversation.

Capricorn Positive Traits

Hard Working.

Maybe it's because Capricorns were born in the wintertime, and what else is there to do but work hard and be patient until springtime comes, right? The Capricorn is ambitious and is always looking at ways to fulfill their life path, unafraid of pursuing new paths and talking to new people. They do it in a subtle way, naturally motivated, that isn't overbearing. They aren't necessarily success-driven, but the Capricorn isn't afraid of working hard to get what they want.

Problem Solvers

Capricorn is a natural problem solver. They find realistic solutions for simple-to-complex issues that truly work. They are driven, calm, and level-headed, which helps with their ability to look for facts and eventually make decisions.

Creative

Capricorn doesn't get a lot of credit for their creativity and instead are most known for their amazing problem-solving skills. Creative doesn't always equate to painting a picture or building a dresser, but the Capricorn is creative in the way they command a room. They are structured communicators and are psychologically able to organize people. They also will surprise you when they pull out an elaborate wedding cake they baked and decorated or show you the manuscript for a murder mystery they wrote.

Capricorn Negative Traits

Pessimistic

Capricorns need someone in their life who is positive and trustworthy, otherwise they fall in step to their cynical ways. They are self-critical, which doesn't help since they are perfectionists. No matter how much you praise a Cap, they will find fault.

Hardheaded

Capricorns don't do gray areas, and instead see life in black or white. They like facts, not fluff. They'd rather not rely on anyone else because of their trust issues and their strong, independent ways. Their stubbornness is defined by the fact that they will rarely reach out for help and will instead struggle.

Distrusting
It's difficult to gain a Capricorn's trust because they are naturally guarded. Although they can read a room, they don't want to be an obvious read. Once you gain their trust, you have a loyal friend for life.

Capricorn Keywords

Capricorn Communication Style

Capricorns don't want to do small talk; instead, they want to get to the point and work on the follow-through of what's next. Small talk creates anxiety for a Capricorn. The best way to communicate with a Capricorn is to stay focused, be clear and direct, and stay away from chit-chat and flowery language.

Capricorn Misconceptions

Capricorns are often seen as boring and serious. It's not so much that the Capricorn is shy, self-centered, or standoffish, it's that they require others to prove themselves. Once they do, the Capricorn shows their fun side and sense of humor.

Don't Be a Capricorn, Capricorn

People get hurt but you get even, Capricorn. If grudges were an Olympic sport, you'd win a gold medal every single time. It's a knee-jerk reaction to be guarded and throw insults and intelligent snarkiness. Capricorn, your lesson is to realize we all make mistakes and forgiveness doesn't mean accepting or excusing the behavior—it's about letting go and realizing we're all human. Even you, Cap.

Thoughts from a Capricorn

A Friend

Capricorns really want to be loved and to have a group of friends around them as loyal as they will be to their friends.

> "Capricorns are very trustworthy, loyal, and they love deeply with their whole heart and soul. They can be stubborn and think they're always right but will admit if they're not. We want to be liked by everyone but think no one likes us. Caps are very friendly and love people but hate drama. They will always help a friend in need and will be loyal for a lifetime."
>
> —Linda

Percy Perfectionist

The Capricorn will cross their t's and dot their i's, double-checking it over and over, until they are stressed and snarky.

> "Capricorns are independent and strong-willed. They are perfectionists and often find themselves frustrated and exhausted; overachievers in work and in play. Many people think that we are closed-minded, but it's because we know we can be loyal to a fault and are afraid of being hurt."
>
> —Kelly

A Pirate's Treasure

Capricorns are much like a pirate's treasure. You have to study the map, proceed with caution, and once you find the treasure you are rewarded with more than the gold—you are rewarded with pride in the quest.

> "Good Ole Capricorn here. We are stubborn and people either love or hate us, there's rarely an in-between. Many don't know that although the exterior appears hard, it's like an eggshell and can be cracked open easily; filled with lots of love and trust that Caps have buried deep down."
>
> —Joy

Capricorn and Relationships

Strengths

Once you've won a Capricorn's heart, they stay committed to promises and vows. The Cap doesn't expect much if you stay loyal. Communication with a Cap needs to be worthwhile and engaging.

Ask for advice. Make them laugh. Appreciate the time they give you. Those small things will help win over the Cap.

Challenges

Capricorns are emotionally closed off, and it takes a while for them to let someone in to make a connection. The fear of being vulnerable and being hurt outweighs the positive of being loved. It's a constant inner conflict. It can make them look aloof and indifferent even if they are feeling the complete opposite.

Capricorn in the Workplace

Strengths

Capricorns are determined and self-assured personalities. They take being a superior seriously and will want their peers and their employees to do the same. They aren't out to climb the corporate ladder as much as they are to always maintain stellar performance. If they see their employees not taking their work as seriously, then there will be consequences.

Challenges

The Capricorn boss isn't ever fun and games. They command in a firm and authoritarian way. You'll likely not find this boss sympathetic and they won't find your excuses, no matter how serious they are, worthy.

Parenting a Capricorn Child

Strengths

Focused: Capricorn children are practical and really don't want to hang around on a Saturday morning with a bunch of kids they don't want to spend time with. The Cap would rather have an itinerary and goal-oriented activity to do. This helps to contain their anxiety and allow them to flourish.

Responsible: Capricorn children are responsible and love to have a job to do. Better yet, offer an allowance with each chart and show them how to invest their money wisely. Just be careful to let your child be a child, as Caps tend to grow up quickly. They appear serious and bashful.

Nature-loving: Your Capricorn will love to be outside and daydreaming by the lake or in the woods. They love to be around animals, digging their hands in the dirt, or jumping in the lake for a swim.

Challenges

Stubborn: The Capricorn is mature out of the womb, and that maturity can become stubbornness as the Cap thinks they know just as much as their elders. They'd prefer to not be parented, which is obviously exactly what they need.

Overthinkers: Overthinking and overanalyzing to the point of depression and stress is a trait that Capricorn has. No matter how many compliments you might give, the insecurity is a built-in trait.

Loner: Capricorn loves their friends and family, but they also have a loner quality and love to be by themselves. Sometimes they just need to get away from everyone and everything to take a break from the hurried life. Sometimes they need some extra love and attention when they go into loner mode.

Capricorn as a Parent

Strengths

Ambitious: The Capricorn is ambitious and teaches their children to be independently motivated. Although they may help with the science project, they won't do the science project, wanting their child to find their own successes.

Respectful: The Capricorn parent requires there to be respect from their children, and in return will offer respect and space like they wanted in their own childhood.

Financially Sound: Logic when it comes to money is very important to a Capricorn. They want to show their family how to save and spend wisely. Although they occasionally splurge, they try to keep balanced, which makes for a financial worry-free household.

Challenges

Restrained: Capricorns are cautious about who they allow into their circle and can take time before they feel comfortable enough around someone to *truly* open up.

Odd Sense of Humor: The Capricorn has a dry and brutally sarcastic sense of humor. Some may even see their humor to be weird, but it's in an intelligent and fun way—only kids won't see it until they get older.

Bossy: So a Capricorn may call it disciplined, but it's truly bossy. They have strong likes and dislikes and can be unmovable on their views.

Capricorn and Finances

Capricorns aren't afraid of hard work and know that hard work will help their bank account grow as well, especially later in life. That doesn't mean that the Capricorn won't spend any money. In fact, they try to balance the saving and the over-spending in a very adult way.

Moon in Capricorn

This is a super time for you to look over your goals, resolutions, and intentions and spend time thinking and meditating on new beginnings rather than what hasn't been working for you. So don't beat yourself up if you were going to organize your sock drawer and instead get caught up on your favorite television episodes—there is still time to make a magical transformation! Tummy issues, lack of energy, and anxiety seem to be issues during the Capricorn energy, which might make it harder for you to feel like creating a vision. Do it anyhow.

New Moon in Capricorn

You may notice a deep sense of sadness and feel lethargic. You may even be questioning your life intentions, and second-guessing your life group—friends, coworkers, work, spouse, and so on, and wondering where you are going and how they might be helping or hurting. The best way to work your way out of this somberness is to look at your dreams, aspirations, how you want your life to look and make small goals as to how that can be accomplished. The Capricorn moon is all about saying, "Hey, I chose that, and I can choose something else," rather than moping and pouting about what hasn't happened.

What you may see during the Capricorn New Moon phase:
>   A boost of energy.
>   Spouting sarcasm.
>   Feeling untrusting.
>   Overthinking.
>   Being able to problem-solve a situation
>   that you've been stuck on.

Full Moon in Capricorn

Have you ever put on your high beams while it was foggy? Instead of helping you see, it causes a glare and compromises your sight. The Capricorn moon energy is a bit like being stuck in the middle of a Stephen King movie, with mist and fury. This is the time to work on trust issues and look hard at the core group of people that surround you. You will find an awakening of sorts, as if a wizard came down and handed you a secret map to help navigate the foggy roads by focusing and trusting in the stars. That way you don't crash into your past or go head-to-head with your made-up monsters of the future.

Soul Work

There's always something you can plant no matter the time of the year. This period doesn't require getting your hands dirty, though; it's planting the seeds of your future. What would you like to grow? The Capricorn energy is grounded and connected to divine inspiration. It's about shifting your perception and seeing the magic already in your life! What is stopping you from doing some of these things now? What can you do to overcome? Which activity will you do first? What do you need to do to make it happen?

Now Is the Time

Do explore your responsibilities and see what needs to be prioritized. Don't dig into your childhood and mourn what was or wasn't. Do create a vision for yourself for the next month. Don't get caught up in a state of somberness. Do get enough sleep, meditation, and exercise. Don't be too disciplined with your routines; add some spontaneity. Do work on forgiving those you think have done you wrong in the past. Don't be too cold and unfeeling—check your emotional temperature.

Capricorn Totem Animal

Elephant

The elephant is a healthy totem for the Capricorn because it teaches the tools for life much like Dumbo and the magic feather. The magic was never in the feather, but in believing in oneself. Capricorns get into the head and try to make sense of the senseless, stay realistic in the realm of superficial. The elephant is graceful and proud, and teaches that with strong will, quiet strength, and pure confidence your dreams can come true.

The elephant offers a gift of:

Strength

Pride

Will

Confidence

Dreams come true

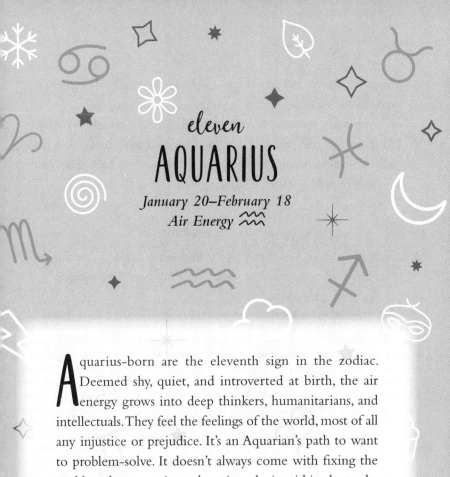

eleven

AQUARIUS

January 20–February 18
Air Energy 〰

A quarius-born are the eleventh sign in the zodiac. Deemed shy, quiet, and introverted at birth, the air energy grows into deep thinkers, humanitarians, and intellectuals. They feel the feelings of the world, most of all any injustice or prejudice. It's an Aquarian's path to want to problem-solve. It doesn't always come with fixing the problem, but sometimes they sit and stir within the problem, pointing fingers and imagining a better place.

The Aquarius enjoys being around a group of like believers who strive to also change the world; they require alone time to reground themselves to keep their aggressive, depressed, and/or moody personality at bay. If there's no healthy balance of life, play, and work, Aquarians can feel so constrained by life that they become miserable and they try to make others around them feel the same way. The saying that misery loves company is very true, especially with the

Aquarius. Be careful to not get caught in their web of negativity and instead send them love and step away for a moment.

Aquarians desire freedom for others, but also themselves. If they don't get that, they feel "less than" and grow cold and shut out those who love them most. The Aquarius will choose to love or accept the love of people who are emotionally less than they deserve.

Aquarius Decans

Each zodiac is broken down into triplicities, each having their own energy added to their zodiac sign. This is Aquarius broken down:

Aquarius of First Decan: January 21–29
Ruled by Uranus.

Positive Energy Traits: This decan is imaginative and creative. They are free thinkers with a high moral compass and believe in the benefit of community. This Aquarius loves social events, especially if it helps with a cause. They are insightful and thoughtful. They like the unusual and aren't afraid to stand out as unique.

Negative Energy Traits: The first decan jumps in and embraces themselves in so many group activities that in order to balance themselves they need to regroup with solitude. Only those close to them will see their depressed mood, as they typically mask it with a pasted smile and a helpful hand. Don't be surprised, however, to see this Aquarius withdraw if they feel any form of confinement—whether a job or a relationship.

Aquarius of Second Decan: January 30–February 8
Ruled by Mercury.

Positive Energy Traits: Enthusiastic and playful, this decan gets bored easily and requires change. This Aquarius is intellectual and excels in academics, soaking up information and trying to continually feel fulfilled. They love to balance a hectic life with lying on the couch to watch a movie and fall asleep. They love social interaction, the inner workings of human psychology, the unknowns of spirituality, and the inner workings of communication.

Negative Energy Traits: If life gets too heavy, this Aquarius hides away. They pretend they can control the stresses of life, but the reality is that they delegate really well; they intellectualize amazingly, but they lack the ability to see things through. They want to problem-solve, but they want someone else to do the work.

Aquarius of Third Decan: February 9–18
Ruled by Venus.

Positive Energy Traits: This decan is sociable and romantic, loves to be loved, and loves to love. This Aquarian is graceful and humanitarian. They want the balance of life and hard work in both their personal world and their career for stability and justice. Their social group is large and everyone is meaningful. It is their natural compassion that makes them a wonderful friend.

Negative Energy Traits: The third decan of Aquarius is impulsive and then must deal with the consequences later. As much as they portray themselves as confident and together, they are mentally neurotic, second-guessing themselves and needing reassurance.

January Aquarius vs. February Aquarius

Along with each sign being split into their third decans, there is a difference between each zodiac split between the months.

January Aquarius is future-oriented.

February Aquarius tries to deal with right now, right here.

January Aquarius loves to hang out with friends.

February Aquarius loves to hang out with friends, but they need their space.

January Aquarius is sarcastic but with a great sense of humor.
February Aquarius is loving.
January Aquarius can be detached.
February Aquarius is emotional.
January Aquarius comes across as aloof when stressed.
February Aquarius lashes out when stressed.
January Aquarius is determined.
February Aquarius is expressive.
January Aquarius doesn't need to stand out and is humbled when they do.
February Aquarius wants to stand out and wants the applause.

Aquarius Masculine and Feminine Energy

Energy has a yin and yang that is interpreted as feminine and masculine, and according to the energy it is explained below:

Feminine January Aquarius: The feminine energy of an Aquarius in January is creative and imaginative with ideas and suggestions. They are competitive, with a quiet and sound command. If there's a problem, this energy will solve it with methodical research, but also with love and caring, in hopes that all parties benefit. They do get bored easily, though, and must be kept busy with multiple jobs and hobbies. There is no such thing as being pulled in too many directions when it comes to this energy. The more on their plate, the happier they are.

Masculine January Aquarius: The masculine energy of an Aquarius in January has a difficult time communicating how they feel or how to ask how others feel. It is because of this that many masculine January Aquarians are labeled narcissistic or cold. To others they portray confidence, but it is done robotically, with lack of emotion. They want to be respected but will criticize others easily. This energy is dignified, intelligent, and forgiving.

It's just that they don't want to be understood, and that can be frustrating.

Feminine February Aquarius: The feminine energy of an Aquarius in February loves to color outside the lines, not wanting to conform to standard society. This energy cares about humanitarian issues, caring more deeply than what many will ever understand. On a personal level this Aquarius detaches effortlessly. They get bored with day-to-day activities and will get bored in romantic relationships and work environments but feel forced to stay loyal and dedicated. It's the complicated, empathic, hopeful, optimistic nature of this energy that often forces them into depression and anxiety. They want so badly to heal the world that they forget they need healing too.

Masculine February Aquarius: The masculine energy of an Aquarius in February is impulsive and curious. They believe their intuition and act upon it without reservation. This energy has a broad view, and always allows for more learning and understanding. This Aquarius is a non-conformist but is polite and dignified. If they disagree with your views, they'll likely walk away with a smile and a shake of the head rather than a heated argument. They are witty, fun to be around, intelligent, and idealistic. It does take a while to get close to this energy as they keep a distance, and even when you've won their trust and their heart, they will still pull away. There's a concern for commitment with them, which makes the saying "it's not you but me" a true statement.

Aquarius Positive Traits

Humanitarian

The Aquarius wants fairness and equality in the world, and often works in their own special way to wake up others to see the way an Aquarian does. They care, and want fairness and love to be the theme, always. They often will step in to help the underdog or to find others that can help the underdog or heal those who need healing. It might be a career choice, or simply involving themselves in their own unique way, or simply listening as someone shares their story. They are big dreamers and believe in progressiveness.

Great Listener

Talking to an Aquarian is never boring. Not only do they have stories to share, but they are generous with a lending, compassionate, and loving ear. With every conversation they come away with knowledge. It's that type of wisdom that helps them offer useful advice, picking up every single detail.

Weird

Aquarius is never dull. They are unique and don't care to fit into a certain group. It's their eccentric and progressive ideas and viewpoints that make people like them. Because their ideas are so different, they are often classified as weird. Even a private person finds themselves confessing to an Aquarius. They have a sexual energy that makes both genders attracted to them. They have a thirst for new opportunities and experiences, and that makes them look fearless.

Aquarius Negative Traits

Rebellious

Aquarius has a rebellious side. Don't you dare tell them what to do. Don't you dare tell them how to think. They love their independent trait even if you don't. If you restrict an Aquarian from being themselves, they will walk away. They aren't afraid of breaking the rules, calling it needed in the name of progress.

Detached

If boredom or repetitive routines set in, you will likely see the Aquarius detach in the name of monotony. Adventure is important, even if in the mental form. Aquarius isn't a fan of stressful situations or anything emotional. They will disappear like a magician, reappearing when life is more steady and calm, whether within them or around them.

Sarcastic

The Aquarius has a mouth they can't control, and it can come across surprisingly sarcastic, and sometimes just plain mean. They are opinionated, especially when upset; all the thoughts they've buried ruthlessly emerge.

Aquarius Keywords

Aquarius Communication Style

Aquarians are students of the zodiac. They love examining the intricacies of humans both consciously and subconsciously. The Aquarius doesn't want fluff, or small talk. They want fun and engaging conversations that aren't too deep. They want to be understood and they want to be stimulated mentally and spiritually, and for that to stir the sexuality of their body, mind, and soul.

Aquarius Misconceptions

An Aquarius Isn't Lazy

Aquarians are often considered lazy. The Aquarius would prefer you not look at it that way, though; they prefer that you understand they need their own private time. They need space to decompress and reground. Sometimes they need assistance and some loving nudges so they don't dive into some depression at great lengths.

Don't Be an Aquarius, Aquarius

You are different, Aquarius, and we all know how much that uniqueness is important to you. One of your positive attributes is that you see things differently, with new, eccentric, and alternative ideas. Your lesson, Aquarius, is to not judge others because they don't see things the way you do and instead embrace you for you, and them for them. When you can do that you become even more beautifully unique.

Thoughts from an Aquarius

Aquarians Move You

Ever changing, the Aquarian doesn't want to be figured out, but they do what's needed to be understood.

"Many believe those born under this sign are amicable and easy going; that we will 'go with the flow,' as it were. But what they fail to see is that we Aquarians are stubborn; think of what moving air can do—the desert is a perfect example, with its moving and shifting dunes. We are tenacious and unrelenting. Just as any wind can be warm, gentle, and encouraging at your back, we can be a cold, icy blast of truthfulness and honesty to your face. Because of the summer of love song 'Age of Aquarius,' we are often confused with the idea of peace. We want to challenge the status quo, to question authority, to make a difference. You may not see the air, but you will feel it and it will move you."

—Sara

It's Hard to Look in the Mirror

Sometimes the things we dislike about another person are the traits we hate within ourselves.

"Growing up I never really paid attention to the zodiac signs, the stars, horoscopes, etc. I thought 'This is just me. Life experiences have made me this way. I am overly emotional, detached, and unpredictable.' These are unfortunately the negative traits of an Aquarius. It wasn't until I was in my late twenties and was more emotionally stable that I was able to recognize these same traits in others; instead of instantly disliking them, I would ask when their birthday was and knew why they were the way they were. It's not that I don't care for Aquarians; I suppose it's just harder for me to like people who have the same traits that I dislike so much about myself. The plus side to an Aquarius is that we are very affectionate, imaginative, creative, loyal, and truthful. It's not all about genetics and experiences. Zodiac signs do play a role. Whether we are ready to realize it. Whether we are open to it. Whether we are ready to accept it. Embrace who you are. Make a daily attempt to love every part of you just as others do!"

—Kristine

A Diamond

Aquarians love to be multifaceted, complex, private—and yet they want others to only see their shiny qualities while hiding imperfections with the sparkle.

"We are imaginative, creative problem-solvers who often see the big picture when others can only visualize the minutia. We are convinced we could save the world if we could figure out how to get everyone else to listen to our often-unconventional solutions. But because we usually can't get everyone aligned with our worldview, we get frustrated. We pull back. We go quiet. When you see descriptions of people born under the sun sign Aquarius as being aloof, detached, or cold, it's often for this reason. We've put forth our best ideas, and too many times those ideas have been shoved aside. Over time, we get so discouraged that we learn to clam up, to shut down, to stop putting forth these wild ideas that could be truly revolutionary if only they were given a chance."

—Kay

Aquarius and Relationships

Strengths

Aquarians love an adventure, and just as quickly love to change the plans in an instant and settle for a movie night at home. An Aquarius loves to love and to be loved. They are sensitive and romantic. They truly want their partner to be their best friend. An Aquarian wants someone who will challenge them and care for them too.

Challenges

An Aquarius gets bored easily and can be fickle if their partner isn't entertaining them in life or in intimacy. The unpredictability, while cute in dating, can be exhausting when it comes to real-life relationships. The other challenge is the Aquarian's withdrawal and pouting times. It's not just that it happens; it happens often.

Aquarius in the Workplace

Strengths

Aquarians are not particularly suited to be bosses. They are impulsive, impatient, get disinterested often, and are quickly frustrated. Although, if your boss is an Aquarius, they are generous and kind-hearted. They make a better coworker or friend than a supervisor.

Challenges

The Aquarius boss likes constant change and improvements, although sometimes the improvements are simply reinventing what isn't even broken. The rules change constantly with an Aquarius boss, and nothing is routine or fixed.

Parenting an Aquarius Child

Strengths

Social: Your Aquarian child loves to socialize with other kids, and they also love to sit down with adults and learn from them. They typically have a lot of friends and love to participate in lots of activities.

Smart: The Aquarius loves to learn and does a pretty great job of staying on top of their academics. They are highly inquisitive and learn by experience.

Helper: Your little Aquarian marches to their own beat, but the rhythm is always helpful and humanitarian. Don't be surprised if your little one wants to donate their birthday gifts or raise money for children with cancer.

Challenges

Absent-Minded: The parent of an Aquarius needs to help their child stay focused. They tend to get bored and derail. They don't love strict schedules and routine, so they do need spontaneity.

Strong-Willed: Don't you dare put limitations on your Aquarius. They don't like to be limited or feel constrained and will rebel if you do. They need their freedom.

Emotional: The Aquarius child can withdraw and become depressed. They need reassurance and constant communication of support. They don't like broken promises and will remember them into adulthood.

Aquarius as a Parent

Strengths

Attached: An Aquarian parent is very attached to their children and will do anything they can to help make a wonderful and enjoyable life for them.

Unique: The Aquarian parent will not be typical or ordinary. They are unique in the way they parent, where vacations take place, and even what food choices are made.

Intuitive: The Aquarian parent is sensitive and intuitive. They will understand more about their child than what their child communicates to them.

Challenges

Withdrawn: Some might see it as sensitivity. Some might see it as depression. Whatever you call it, Aquarians are notoriously known for feeling so much that they must retreat.

Frustrated: Outwardly they may look calm and together, afraid to communicate with anyone about what they are feeling, except maybe sarcasm. It can bring long-term issues such as depression. It can also make the child feel as if they aren't helping to make their parent happy enough.

Rule Breakers: Although the Aquarius parent values the system of education and rules, they rarely stick to the trends of traditions. When everyone else in class is bringing cupcakes for their birthday, the Aquarian parent may simply call it ridiculous and not do it.

Aquarius and Finances

The theme of not wanting to be figured out crawls into an Aquarian's financial picture as well. One day they are all about saving, and the next they are booking a month-long trip to Ireland and then feeling remorseful after the adventure when they look at their bank statement. Then they do it all over again a few months later.

Moon in Aquarius

When the moon is in the sign of Aquarius, your emotions will be extra potent to help you eliminate what isn't serving you well in your life, and to help usher in some newness.

New Moon in Aquarius

This New Moon will take some action on your part. Remember the last time you experienced rejection and felt as if you couldn't even move, but then something fabulous happened and you wondered why you were acting like a lovesick teenager? Well, this New Moon offers you a fresh start. But there's no miracle; there's work and action that can make it so.

The week before this New Moon lends itself to many concerns over financial situations, friendship and family drama, and frustrations that make many feel super emotional. Remember that tomorrow is always another day. You can only do as much as you can. You are human and not super-human.

What You May See during the Aquarius New Moon Phase:
Creativity.
A busy social calendar.
Lending a helping hand.
Pursuing inventive ideas.

Being over emotional and easily annoyed.

Passive-aggressiveness.

Stubbornness.

Full Moon in Aquarius

With the moon being in the sign of Aquarius you will more than likely want to feel free: free from relationships that aren't working, friendships that are stifled, and situations that are making you feel uncomfortable. Over the next couple of days you may feel as if someone or some situation has been strangling you, and you will no longer take it. This is the best time to write out what and who you are upset with and burn or rip it up. Release, cry, stomp up and down—but get it out. Then affirm what you want from others, and water, fertilize, and care for that.

Soul Work

Draw a circle of protection around you by imagining an angel scattering rose petals all around you. You feel the anxiety and negativity wash away. You smell the scent and you feel relaxed immediately. Notice your thoughts, judgments, distractions, and worries disappearing as you feel safe and secure in the ring of petals from heaven. As you reground yourself to your positive thoughts and ideas, ask your angels these questions and then listen: What adventures should I choose right now? What can I do to help the world? What am I avoiding right now? How can I let go of feeling overly sensitive about what I'm avoiding? Thank the angels for their time and take the messages forward.

Now Is the Time

Do spend some time journaling. Don't get passive-aggressive and avoid what needs to be handled. Do look at ways to spend time with a social circle. Don't detach from the people who've always been there for you. Do look at ways to help in a humanitarian way. Don't miss out on opportunities because you are so caught up in "what ifs." Do celebrate your accomplishments. Don't mistake monotony for boredom; everything takes time to grow, even you.

Aquarius Totem Animal

Peacock

Aquarius is a true peacock. Known for their beautiful souls and ability to inspire others, Aquarians are the spiritual incarnation of a brilliant peacock on full display. An Aquarius lets you know who they are up front and doesn't try to hide, nor do they want to hide. Just like a peacock showing his immense, gorgeous train, the Aquarian has a brilliant energy that people are attracted to and enamored with. Peacocks and Aquarians both have a mean streak, though, and will chase anyone down who bothers them.

The peacock offers a gift of:

Integrity

Honor

Compassion

Laughter

Gratitude

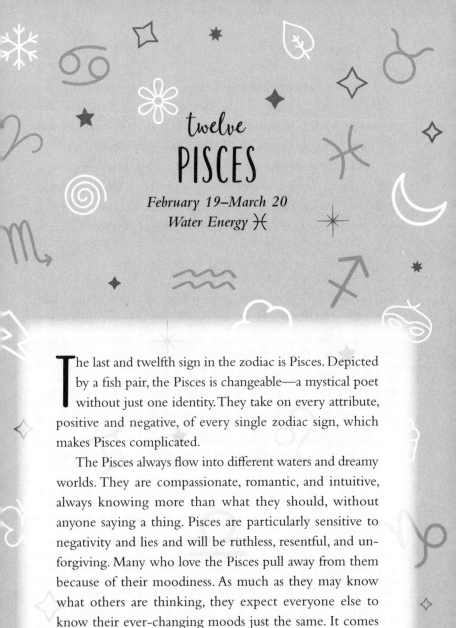

twelve
PISCES

February 19–March 20
Water Energy ♓

The last and twelfth sign in the zodiac is Pisces. Depicted by a fish pair, the Pisces is changeable—a mystical poet without just one identity. They take on every attribute, positive and negative, of every single zodiac sign, which makes Pisces complicated.

The Pisces always flow into different waters and dreamy worlds. They are compassionate, romantic, and intuitive, always knowing more than what they should, without anyone saying a thing. Pisces are particularly sensitive to negativity and lies and will be ruthless, resentful, and unforgiving. Many who love the Pisces pull away from them because of their moodiness. As much as they may know what others are thinking, they expect everyone else to know their ever-changing moods just the same. It comes across as secretive and sometimes manipulative and is done unintentionally; it is hardwired into their makeup.

Pisces are hard on themselves, being their own worst enemies, and take on the happiness of others, a tough and unrealistic job. They constantly battle how they should feel and how they should act, and yet tell others how they should feel and how they should act.

Pisces are indecisive and are daydreamers; they don't always pay attention to what others are saying and often rewrite the past with their own version. They are open-minded, and they do well surrounded by strong, empathic, and confident people.

Pisces Decans

Each zodiac is broken down into triplicities, each having their own energy added to their zodiac sign. This is Pisces broken down:

Pisces of First Decan: February 19–29
Ruled by Neptune.

Positive Energy Traits: This decan is imaginative and creative. They are highly intuitive and caring. They are great managers and are often steps ahead of most. This Pisces is romantic and sensitive, they don't like drama and would prefer stability—if someone else is creating it.

Negative Energy Traits: This Pisces wanders around life not knowing who they are, what they want to be, and pretending that they don't much care, all the while caring. Finances for this Pisces can be summed up as a nightmare. They love their things and they love buying things for not only themselves but others, too, which makes their bank account suffer. They have zero filter and will tell it like it is, even if it hurts your feelings.

Pisces of Second Decan: March 1–10
Ruled by the Moon.

Positive Energy Traits: This Pisces is the giver. They love seeing others happy and that makes them feel happy in return. They are the feelers and the knowers, with an intense personality not everyone understands. They are shy and private, and sometimes closed off, but they don't portray that attribute to be difficult.

Negative Energy Traits: This decan is the expert victim and is good with the emotionally abusive passive communication. A dark and depressed sense of humor, they feel lonely even when people are around. Overly sensitive, this Pisces is often sick— if not physically, then mentally or spiritually.

Pisces of Third Decan: March 11–20
Ruled by Pluto.

Positive Energy Traits: This Pisces has an intense personality and emotions run very deep. Although intuitive, they are less sensitive than the other decans. They are creative, adaptable, and pragmatic in seeing things from a visionary perspective.

Negative Energy Traits: This Pisces lives within their own reality, a head full of unrealistic jealousies and resentments. This decan needs a lot of time to themselves, which makes them seem temperamental and moody.

February Pisces vs. March Pisces

Along with each sign being split into their third decans, there is a difference between each zodiac split between the months.

February Pisces is blunt.

March Pisces will share their truths.

February Pisces rarely moves on when hurt.

March Pisces will move on when hurt but will play with the scars.

February Pisces is laid back.

March Pisces is high maintenance.

February Pisces is fearful and becomes lazy out of fear.

March Pisces is fearful, but it drives them.

February Pisces is good at being a con artist.

March Pisces is good at victimizing themselves.

February Pisces can lie to your face and not feel bad.

March Pisces will lie and feel awful.

February Pisces is arrogant.

March Pisces is compassionate.

February Pisces is real.

March Pisces puts on an act and pretends.

Pisces Masculine and Feminine Energy

Energy has a yin and yang that is interpreted as feminine and masculine, and according to the energy it is explained below:

Feminine February Pisces: The feminine energy of a Pisces in February is gentle and compassionate. Mystical and sensitive, the feminine February Pisces is complicated. One moment quiet and contemplative, the next charming and the life of the party, and the next brooding and depressed.

Masculine February Pisces: The masculine energy of a Pisces in February is fun-loving and spontaneous. They often hide serious situations by adding doses of humor, mostly to protect their own soft heart. Although motivated, this energy doesn't necessarily care about conventional success or financial gain. They are secretive, especially regarding money. It's easy to be suspicious of them because they don't divulge everything; to them details are a waste of time and energy, and details just plain bore them. Romantic and creative, this energy is fun to have as a friend, but is exhausting to have as a romantic partner.

Feminine March Pisces: The feminine energy of a Pisces in March has an unpredictable nature: one moment happy and laughing, the next bitter, critical, and crying. This energy is known for fibbing and creating stories that make them believe everything they've said, making the other party wonder what is true or not. It's hard to trust this Pisces with their fragile nature that makes it hard to get close and love. Yet, what this energy craves most of all is support, fun, and love. This Pisces is a worrier from birth on, and as they get older the worry can turn to depression, especially regarding financial issues.

Masculine March Pisces: The masculine energy of a Pisces in March is put off by negativity and yet may just be the one throwing out the most of it in their world. They want the world to be a better place but can often become lazy and consumed by how it should be done instead of just making changes to get it done. They are good with money, balancing, and budgeting. Sensitive, they take things at face value. Although they do have a sense of intuition, they attempt to rationalize it with black-and-white details and work best under a routine. This energy would prefer to live as simply as possible, not consumed with senseless worry and stresses.

Pisces Positive Traits

Creative

The Pisces is imaginative and creative. It doesn't always equate to painting a picture or working as an interior designer. They don't live in a black-and-white world; they see and feel in color. They offer the world unique views, imagination, and a dreamy outlook on life. They want to understand others and the way they tick.

Laid Back

Carefree, the Pisces is laid back and doesn't want to get hung up on details. They are easy-going and flexible. They rarely hold grudges and will forgive. The Pisces sees all sides of the story, which often makes it difficult to make decisions, but it also helps them stay neutral with others.

Curious

The Pisces loves to learn, research, and explore. They like to learn about people, their inner workings, and explore ideas. You may find a Pisces digging through biographies or watching documentaries, always searching for knowledge and exploring information.

Pisces Negative Traits

Impatient

Although easy-going, the Pisces is impatient, especially if it has anything to do with time. They don't like waiting and they require the world to work on the Pisces timeline. Anything other than that is unacceptable. The restlessness makes them angry and feel disrespected.

Moody

The Pisces mood shifts from happy to miserable with the snap of a finger. They are finely attuned to the energies of others through their intuitive and empathic gifts. It's like they're a sponge and can chameleon through others' moods. Not complicated or anything.

Daydreamer

Pisces want to save the world. They find the broken and put their all into fixing them, then get frustrated when it is assumed that their advice is judgmental. They assume that things can happen at the snap of a finger and get upset with others when they share the reality of the situation. It's maddening for everyone, including the Pisces.

Pisces Keywords

Pisces Communication Style

A Pisces can be on and just as quickly turn themselves off. They might invite you to their home for a dinner party, and then withdraw alone to do the dishes in the kitchen or watch a television show in the den. As social as a Pisces might want to be, they are just as introverted. The conversation must stay imaginative and dreamy, but as soon as it turns serious, they're out.

Pisces Misconceptions

Pisces hardly have a filter, and because of their open opinions, it comes across as judgmental. The Pisces sees things the way they want to see it. They are intuitive and see things clearer than most. They are smart and know more than they get credit for. So, when they offer suggestions or advice, it is meant to be caring. They want the best of the best for everyone—they don't mean it in a judgmental way as much as it may sound that way; they are just honest to a fault.

Don't Be a Pisces, Pisces

Don't stop dreaming, Pisces. Your head-in-the-clouds attribute is endearing, but you do have to join the real world sometimes. You do things your way almost all the time, withdrawing whether you are happy or sad. In your head you have the best fights, but rarely share any of those thoughts. You may want to fight and scream, share and fix, but instead life goes unresolved. Your lesson, Pisces, is that life can be easier if you stop ignoring the issues in life and learn how to better communicate.

Thoughts from a Pisces

The Flow of Life

Pisces have a perception of what life should look like and it rarely is the way it is. They go with the flow until the frustration sets in and they withdraw and grow moody.

> "I am a friendly person, always drawn to unique and intelligent people. I'm sensitive and need my down time because I am the magnet to everyone everywhere

wanting to tell me their life story and in need of advice. Sometimes it gets to be too much, but I go with the flow anyway until I can explore an outlet. Pisces love the water and music, good food and the arts. Anything that feels good, smells good, tastes good, and is good—it's why we can become depressed, because life isn't always good. In the world of Pisces, we want it to be, though. We see how it could be and then we see how it is and get frustrated. It's not that we want to be difficult; we just don't always want to participate in this world, and we don't have the energy in changing the world to be the way we see it should be."

—Sam

Happy to Be a Pisces

Pisces are often taken advantage of because of their kind hearts, and because of this they can feel vulnerable and bitter. Learning how to balance the Pisces and only give to those who deserve it will help the Pisces continue to stay happy to be a Pisces.

"I can't imagine being anything other than a Pisces. I've always loved everything about the water. I think of myself as a mermaid in spirit. When I think of being a Pisces or anything Piscean, I think: gratitude, familiarity, comfort. It just seems right. My Piscean nature connects me with nature and spirit. My head is in the clouds, as it were, and that's fine. I am psychic, intuitive, and an empath. I have always been in tune with the astral, the dream world. I've been using crystals, the tarot, and other so-called New Age tools to access my subconscious and communicate with 'the other' for decades, and I can share these spiritual, metaphysical thoughts and experiences with others in a positive way."

—Regan

Best of the Last

The final sign of the zodiac wheel takes on all the positive and negative attributes of all the other astrological signs, making Pisces complicated and amazing in twelve different ways.

"I am the final sign in the zodiac circle. Imagine: You walk around the block, writing down one or two things about each house you pass, Aries being the starting house. By the time you reach my home, you would have picked up a little info of each of the other homes. That's me. I have a visible trait of each of the other signs. My head may seem 'up in the clouds' but that's only because I'm planning my week, the grocery list, the vacation for my family with the money I've saved each paycheck. I seem intuitive because I am a little bit of everyone. I love being a Pisces. I love being me."

—Dayna

Pisces and Relationships

Strengths

A Pisces is a supportive, compassionate, and loving partner. They love to offer advice (even if they don't like to take advice themselves). They are intuitive and accurate with life situations, having a good handle on reading others. The Pisces loves to travel and explore, experiencing all the beauty the world can offer. The more colorful and less realistic the better. Being loved by a Pisces is a gift. They are sensitive and often selfless. Pisces do need to be cared for in a gentle way and require loyalty, dedication, honesty, and tact. They love to be loved, are sexual, and are snugglers. They love family and traditions and will put the ones they love above themselves.

Challenges
The Pisces make themselves vulnerable by the way they love. If it isn't reciprocated, then they become manipulative and scary angry. If they are lied to or betrayed, they will be vengeful and vindictive. The Pisces needs alone time and plenty of it. If they don't get enough, then they will be moody and lash out. They are indecisive and their mind tends to wander, so don't expect them to hear everything in your conversation. They don't like anything connected to reality and stress if it deals with finances or illnesses and will put imaginary headphones on. Look for a lot of pouting if they don't get enough time with you.

Pisces in the Workplace

Strengths
The Pisces as a boss uses their skills in every creative way, no matter the industry or business. They help the staff to better understand one another. They are hard workers, supportive, and like to inspire. They aren't the best bosses, though, as they are sensitive and don't want to be authoritative figures, although they believe they are great leaders. They'd rather not be in the spotlight unless they choose to be.

Challenges
The Pisces boss doesn't like rules, and they get easily bored with the day-to-day tasks. They get overwhelmed easily and become moody and can become aggressive, withdrawing.

Parenting a Pisces Child

Strengths

Gentle Souls: The Pisces child is a gentle soul. They are caring and compassionate, loving and thoughtful. They try to not get in the way, doing well keeping themselves busy. Make certain to be kind to them, but truthful too.

Passionate: Pisces finds something they're interested in and it will keep them focused and occupied. Whether a toy or an activity, there's a sense of loyalty from birth on with a Pisces, and their choices are meaningful. If they are acting moody or bored, help them find that passion.

Daydreamers: Pisces children see things in technicolor and need to embrace drawing, writing, dancing, music, acting, a sport, or anything else creative or imaginative. You'll likely see them more excited about an extracurricular activity than a scholastic one, although they are intelligent.

Challenges

Sensitive: Sensitive Pisces take everything to heart, even the things that have nothing to do with them. It's important to communicate with the Pisces, reassuring and expressing your love. They aren't fragile, they are just sensitive and concerned about everyone else's happiness, sometimes forgetting about their own.

Manipulative: The Pisces loves to run away from their problems. If they failed a test, you'll likely find it bunched up in the bottom of their backpack without a word from your little one. If it's not bunched up in the bottom of their backpack, you'll likely get a call from the teacher wondering when you started signing paperwork with a crayon. They don't like to disappoint and will avoid facing real-life issues.

Daydreamers: A Pisces child is imaginative and a dreamer. They don't much like micromanaging or authoritative figures, wanting instead to be respected like a peer. The Pisces teenager feels as if they need to fight the system, and this can make them embrace an addictive personality. The cause is often attributed to being the last in the zodiac, much like a pup in a litter who has to fight for food.

Pisces as a Parent

Strengths

Nurturing: The Pisces parent is nurturing and caring, wanting to provide emotional support for their child. Many times, they take what they didn't receive in their own childhood and offer that and more to their own children.

Encouraging: The Pisces parent gives lots of imaginative freedom and will encourage their child to be their own unique self. They are loving and caring, not afraid of spoiling their child if it helps direct them to their wants, needs, and passions.

Fun: The Pisces parent is the fun parent. Rules? What rules? Bedtime? Nope. Want to skip school? Sure. They don't love rules in their own life and will rarely impose regulations on their child. Now, there're negatives and positives with this if the child requires a strict parent.

Challenges

Unrealistic: The Pisces parent wants to spend time with their kids and is unrealistic and sometimes unhealthy with the needs and wants they put on their kids.

Depressed: The Pisces is an introvert and moody. When they are overwhelmed with life circumstances they withdraw. Although normally carefree, they do go into a doom-and-gloom state more than others. They will isolate themselves, even their own children.

Narcissist: It's really all about what a Pisces wants and how it feeds their needs. They will play victim and hold it against anyone and everyone, including their children. It's often fueled from their own insecurity and lack of self-worth.

Pisces and Finances

Pisceans don't care much about the money they earn so long as their mission is right on track and their conscience is clear. February Pisceans tend to struggle with saving and would be happiest if they could be a philanthropist. March Pisceans worry about not having enough. No matter how money is being made, Pisces representatives can earn easily thanks to their energy, imagination, and creativity.

Moon in Pisces

Pisces is the twelfth sign of the zodiac, and it is a spunky energy. During this moon energy, you will likely be even more of a psychic sponge. You are already a sponge to energy, but you will feel even heavier when the moon is anywhere near Pisces. A bit snarky, this energy will likely have you mumbling under your breath your true feelings about everything and anyone. Truths have a way of being revealed under the Pisces moons that can be hurtful and insightful, but also healing once worked through.

With the moon visiting the sign of Pisces, it can awaken your intuitive side. Dreams might be a bit more intense, with symbolism and messages that you need to pay close attention to. Your animals may react to things unseen. You may feel like you've just had it, burned out with life and then some.

New Moon in Pisces

The Piscean New Moon spotlights the creative, fun, and romantic personality within you. You might notice yourself feeling lazy (relaxed) and not wanting to do anything but daydream, nap, read a book, play on Facebook, and so on. Past drama might be dredged up in your mind along with a feeling of being unjustified. This is when it is a good time to not just push that aside but throw it away and realize that the past is the past and the hands of the clock go forward, not back.

What to expect during the Pisces New Moon:

Finding humor to push away the sorrow.
Enhanced creativity.
Festering in past issues.
Being overly emotional.

Full Moon in Pisces

Pay attention to the lessons that are being revealed to you. These are messages to release, not analyze and obsess over. This insight is to help you heal, release, and move forward. Be careful to not get caught up in those who want to cause drama and trip you as you journey through your own healing.

Soul Work

Pisces energy often has us review the past heartaches. During the moon energy it's time to release the past. Send back misfortunes and injustice to the person you feel has sent it your way. Light a white candle in front of a small mirror and dab the four corners of the mirror with vinegar. With the mirror reflecting the flame, you can call on your guides and angels and simply say, "With the help of the moon, make _____ realize soon that any harm or misery cursed be returned and reversed." You are not sending harm to that person; you are simply returning what was done to you.

Now Is the Time

Do explore your creative side. Don't be gullible. Do some journaling. Don't be too clingy. Do reach out to family and friends that you've been feeling drawn to connect (or reconnect) with. Don't be a cosmic sponge and absorb other people's negative energy. Do go shopping and buy yourself something pretty. Don't forget how powerful you are.

Pisces Totem Animal

Wolf

Wolves are highly intuitive and loyal. The energy of the wolf needs a loyal and interesting romance that ebbs and flows with their varying moods. They feel complete with their pack of family around them and will nurture them. The wolf energy is a source of lunar power, seeing more and knowing more than others. The wolf is a guardian and an ally. Although many are frightened by the wolf, they are reasonable, even if they might nip, growl, and sometimes bite. The wolf pretends they don't care, or that they are independent, but the reality is they feel deeply and love passionately. The lesson for the wolf is to learn how to communicate clearly, trust the intuition, and stay motivated.

The wolf offers a gift of:

Loyalty

Intelligence

Intuition

Instinct

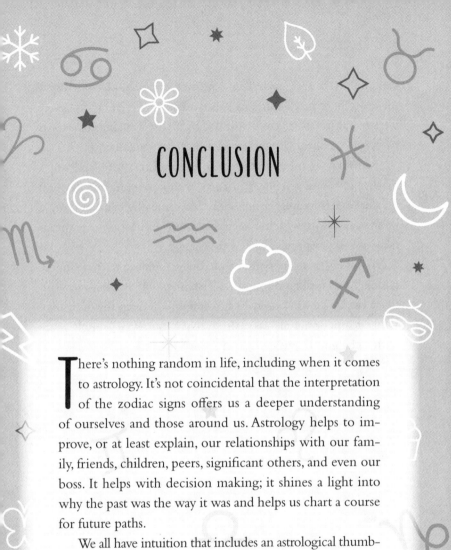

CONCLUSION

There's nothing random in life, including when it comes to astrology. It's not coincidental that the interpretation of the zodiac signs offers us a deeper understanding of ourselves and those around us. Astrology helps to improve, or at least explain, our relationships with our family, friends, children, peers, significant others, and even our boss. It helps with decision making; it shines a light into why the past was the way it was and helps us chart a course for future paths.

We all have intuition that includes an astrological thumbprint. It doesn't mean anyone needs to display a flashy "Psychic" or "Astrologer" sign because intuition comes from within us, around us, and from past experiences. Information from the zodiac teaches us what to do, where to go, and who to trust. It might not be a complete road map but it's an outline. We often want exact turn-by-turn directions, but even then we doubt and create false scenarios in our head, especially if there is a lot of gray around us. When a knowing can't be explained, we attempt to rationalize it. Astrology is a blueprint, keys that open twelve doors filled with information and abundant discoveries.

Astrology should be treated as inspiration, a tool, and not a black-and-white science. You can't change people, but through greater understanding, compassion, and sympathy you can change your perception, which can make a shift. Just looking at things from a new perspective can create change.

Astrology is an investment in your happiness, deeper understanding, and healing through understanding of the language. With those twelve keys, it's up to you whether you open the doorways. So next time someone asks you "What's your sign?" simply reply with "The good sign."

ASTROLOGICAL TERMS

Air signs: There are four astrological elements—water, fire, air, and earth. Libra, Aquarius, and Gemini are all air signs. People who are air signs tend to appear emotionally detached and analytical. They often lead with their mind rather than their heart but have an amazing level of creativity and sensitivity.

Aquarius: Those born between January 20 and February 18.

Aries: Those born between March 21 and April 19.

Ascendant: The "ascendant" (or "rising sign"—these terms are used interchangeably) refers to the sign that is "rising" or is on the eastern horizon at the time of birth.

Autumn equinox: Occurs in September and is connected to gathering harvest and conserving your resources.

Birthchart: A diagram showing the exact positioning of the planets in the signs at the moment of birth.

Cancer: Those born between June 21 and July 22.

Capricorn: Those born between December 22 and January 20.

Cardinal signs: Refers to the astrological signs of Aries, Cancer, Libra, and Capricorn. These signs are associated with the start of a new season—spring, summer, fall, and winter, and represent new beginnings.

Cusp: The line dividing the twelve zodiac signs.

Decanate: Each sign is divided into three equal parts of 10 degrees.

Earth signs: There are four astrological elements—water, fire, air, and earth. Earth signs are Taurus, Virgo, and Capricorn.

Eclipse: When the sun and the moon intersect in their paths around the earth. These include solar eclipses (when the moon casts a shadow on the earth) and lunar eclipses (when the earth casts a shadow on the moon). Eclipses bring about changes and are usually tied to a certain theme.

Elements: There are four elements of the zodiac: fire, earth, air, and water. The signs of the same element often share qualities of their like element.

Equinox: This is when the center of the sun lines up with the Earth's equator. It signifies the beginning of spring and fall.

Feminine Signs: Taurus, Cancer, Virgo, Scorpio, Capricorn, and Pisces.

Fire signs: Aries, Leo, and Sagittarius.

Fixed signs: Taurus, Leo, Scorpio, and Aquarius.

Gemini: People born between May 21 and June 21.

Houses: A birthchart is divided into twelve sections, called houses. Each house represents a different experience or energy.

Jupiter: This planet is associated with luck, leisure, wealth, intellect, and optimism.

Leo: People born between July 23 and August 22.

Libra: People born between September 23 and October 23.

Luna: The Moon.

Masculine signs: Aries, Gemini, Leo, Libra, Sagittarius, and Aquarius. Those born under the masculine signs can be seen as assertive and confident.

Mercury: This planet is associated with communication, logic, reasoning, restlessness, and opinions.

Mercury in retrograde: When Mercury is in retrograde it's as if the planet goes into sleep mode. Because Mercury is the ruler of communication, electronics, shipping, and travel, many related things can be disrupted and cause frustration to our daily lives.

Mutable signs: Gemini, Virgo, Sagittarius, and Pisces. Those born under mutable signs are often seen as more flexible.

Natal chart: The natal chart refers to a chart for the time of birth.

Opposition: An opposition is when planets are exactly opposite each other in the chart wheel. Oppositions create stress and anxiety.

Pisces: People born between February 19 and March 20.

Planetary return: When a planet in transit returns to the position it was at when a person was born.

Polarity: Each sign has a relationship with another sign. Opposite signs have a polarized relationship.

Retrograde: If a planet is in retrograde on your birthchart, you may feel the energy portrayed by that planet in a deeper way.

Rising sign: "Ascendant" or "rising sign" are used interchangeably. This is the sign that was rising on the eastern horizon at the time of birth.

Rulership: Different signs are "ruled" by different planets. Those planets then influence the different signs.

Sagittarius: People born between November 22 and December 21.

Scorpio: People born between October 24 and November 22.

Solstice: This occurs twice a year, at the beginning of summer and winter. The longest or shortest days of the year. The summer solstice occurs in June and is connected to abundance and harvest. The winter solstice occurs in December and helps us see light in our life through the darkness.

Spring equinox: The spring equinox, in March, is associated with new beginnings.

Sun sign: Your zodiac sign according to the day and month you were born.

Taurus: People born between April 20 and May 20.

Transit: The study of where planets might be in the future and how they may change aspects.

Uranus: This planet represents unexpected disruptions and sudden catastrophes.

Virgo: People born between August 23 and September 22.

Water element: There are four astrological elements—water, fire, air, and earth. Water signs are emotional and have amazing intuition.

Water Signs: Cancer, Scorpio, and Pisces.

Zodiac: From the Greek word *zodiakos*, which means "circle of animals." It's divided into twelve signs, and acts as a gauge for personality traits.

To Write to the Author

If you wish to contact the author or would like more information about this book, please write to the author in care of Llewellyn Worldwide Ltd. and we will forward your request. Both the author and the publisher appreciate hearing from you and learning of your enjoyment of this book and how it has helped you. Llewellyn Worldwide Ltd. cannot guarantee that every letter written to the author can be answered, but all will be forwarded. Please write to:

Kristy Robinett
⁄ Llewellyn Worldwide
2143 Wooddale Drive
Woodbury, MN 55125-2989
Please enclose a self-addressed stamped envelope for reply,
or $1.00 to cover costs. If outside the U.S.A., enclose
an international postal reply coupon.

Many of Llewellyn's authors have websites with additional information and resources. For more information, please visit our website at http://www.llewellyn.com.